CW00518164

Find Your

COSMIC
CALLING

A Guide to Discovering Your Life's Work with

A S T R O L O G Y

Natalie Walstein

FAIR WINDS

Inspiring | Educating | Creating | Entertaining

Brimming with creative inspiration, how-to projects, and useful information to enrich your everyday life, Quarto Knows is a favorite destination for those pursuing their interests and passions. Visit our site and dig deeper with our books into your area of interest: Quarto Creates, Quarto Cooks, Quarto Homes, Quarto Lives, Quarto Drives, Quarto Explores, Quarto Gifts, or Quarto Kids.

First Published in 2022 by Fair Winds Press, an imprint of The Quarto Group, 100 Cummings Center, Suite 265-D, Beverly, MA 01915, USA.
T (978) 282–9590 F (978) 283–2742 QuartoKnows.com

Fair Winds Press titles are also available at discount for retail, wholesale, promotional, and bulk purchase. For details, contact the Special Sales Manager by email at specialsales@quarto.com or by mail at The Quarto Group, Attn: Special Sales Manager, 100 Cummings Center, Suite 265-D, Beverly, MA 01915, USA.

26 25 24 23 22   1 2 3 4 5

ISBN: 978–0–7603–7279–1

Digital edition published in 2022
eISBN: 978–0–7603–7280–7

Library of Congress Cataloging-in-Publication Data

Walstein, Natalie, author.
Find your cosmic calling : a guide to uncovering your life's work
  with astrology / by Natalie Walstein.
ISBN 9780760372791 (hardcover) | ISBN 9780760372807 (ebook)
1. Quality of life. 2. Astrology.
CLCC HN25 .W46 2022 (print) | LCC HN25 (ebook) | DDC 133.5–dc23

LCCN 2021029154 (print) | LCCN 2021029155 (ebook)

Design and Page Layout: Laura Klynstra
Illustrations: Abby Diamond | @Finchfight

Printed in China.

For you,
a shining star
who was born
on this Earth to
do amazing
things

Contents

CHAPTER 1

What Is a Cosmic Calling?

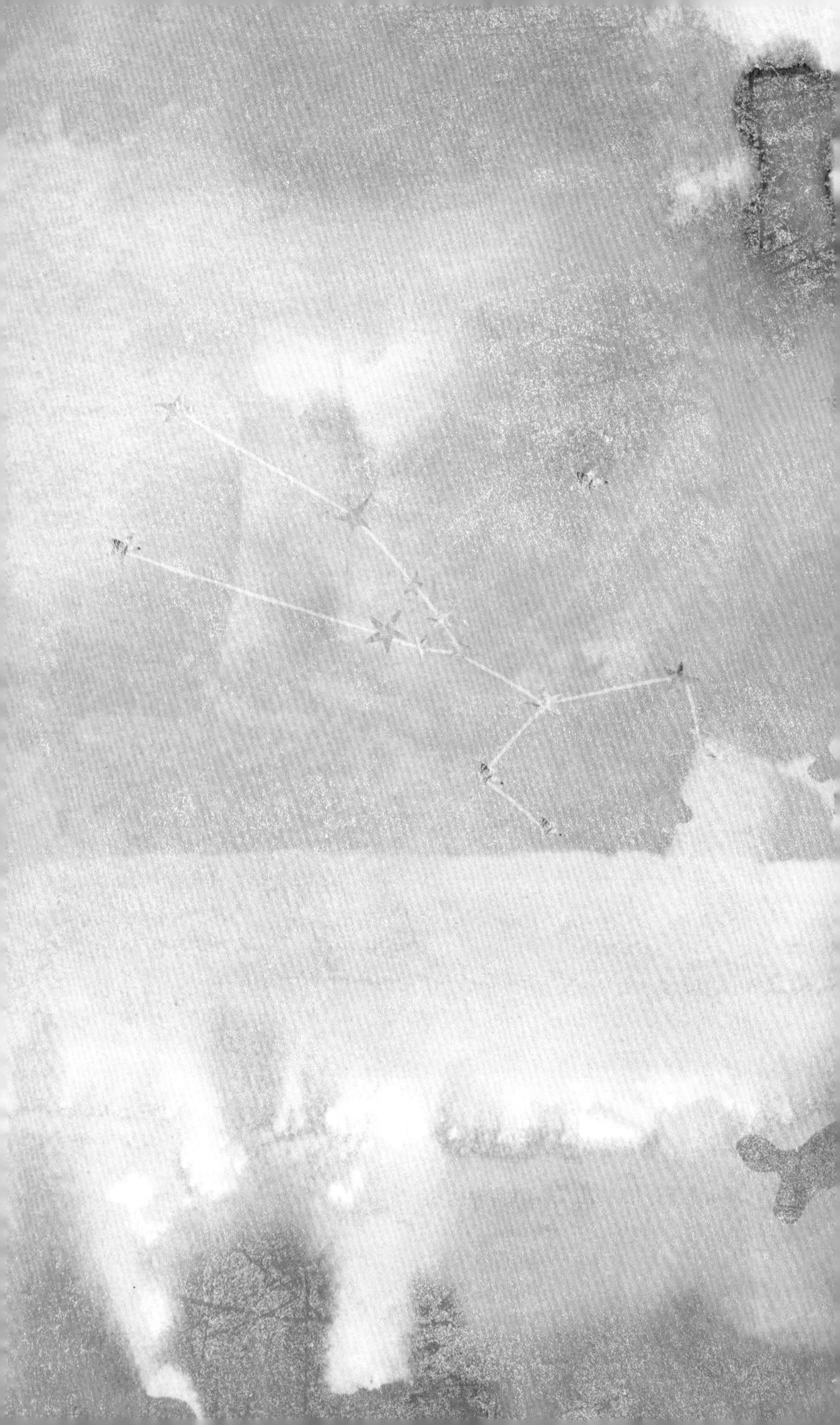

"What am I really here to do with my life?" is a question that many of us ask ourselves at one point or another. It is easy to look around and see that the world could use our help, yet it's often difficult to determine what we can do personally to create positive ripples of change in the way that feels most in alignment to us. This all begins to shift when you know why you are here and what you were born to do.

Now, thanks to the modernization of the ancient wisdom of astrology, finding your true calling has become less complicated than ever before! In this book, you will discover how to read your own astrology chart. This powerful star map of your soul can help you tap into your unique gifts and harness your best skills and talents to leave behind a lasting impact that is purposeful and rewarding. Whether you are feeling unfulfilled with your current work, getting ready to start a business, or looking to follow new dreams in retirement, you will discover how to share your unique energy with the world in an enjoyable way that calls to you on a more meaningful soul level.

As each planet and point unravels a new layer of meaning and insight into the grander plan the cosmos has in store for you, dreams and desires will be validated, inner workings will be demystified, and deeper soul-level insights will be gained. You will be able to better understand yourself, the people around you, and the greater potential of your life's work that has secretly been calling to you all along.

How to Use This Book

This book was designed to take you on a cosmic journey through your astrology chart. On the way, you can uncover the blueprint behind your life purpose so you can more mindfully determine who you really are and what you were born to do. In a way, you can choose your own adventure. Each section is meant to be read with a copy of your astrology chart handy so you can seek out the interpretations that apply to you based on where the planets and points fall on your chart. The process of finding and calculating your chart is laid out step by step in the section How to Read Your Astrology Chart (see page 15).

If you choose to read all the interpretations instead of only the ones that apply to you, you will learn a great deal about the range of human archetypal behaviors and their characteristics. We are all wired in a completely unique manner depending on where in the sky the planets and other points were when we were born. Seeing this may make it easier to accept and appreciate others' differences. Taking in the limitless combinations of energies that one can be born with may also help you acknowledge how special it is to have ended up being who you are.

After you have decoded your cosmic calling, you may wish to use this book as an ongoing resource for finding out more about the people around you. Reading and decoding the charts of others will allow you to better understand and appreciate their needs and differences, whether these are people you live with or work closely with. It is much easier to collaborate with and have compassion for another person when you can see into their soul, determine what makes them tick, and encourage them to do what lights them up most. If only we could all be so lucky to have a friend like that!

What Is a Cosmic Calling?

Many of us spend our lives living on autopilot, letting the outside world guide us and override our own inner knowledge. That's how we end up working in jobs we hate for years—or even decades—and basing our idea of success on what other people have accomplished rather than what we, deep down, truly desire in our heart. It's easy to lose ourselves in pleasing others when we are not tuned in to and aware of our own needs, desires, and passions. That is part of why it is so important to tap into your cosmic calling.

Your cosmic calling is what you were born on this earth to pursue. It's your soul's mission and your life's work. It is comprised of your soul's gifts, what fulfills you on an emotional level and a spiritual level, your role in this world, and how to accomplish greater levels of success in alignment with your true desires, motivations, and dream for the future. You can discover your cosmic calling by reading your astrology chart and decoding the placement of each planet in the sky when you were born.

Your astrology chart, which contains a map of the solar system at the exact date, time, and location of your birth, is like your soul's blueprint. Your cosmic calling is one of the things you can come to understand by decoding this blueprint. Overall, no matter who you are, your cosmic calling is the same as everyone's: to embrace your natural-born gifts while overcoming the challenges that stand in the way of following the plan your soul has created for you. That plan is exactly what we will be seeking to explore and uncover in this book.

CAREER VS. CALLING

In today's world, the meanings of the words *career* and *calling* are not always aligned. Our lives are spent working and trying to get ahead so we can make a living, whereas our personal and spiritual development is often seen as something that would be "nice to have" instead of a top priority. Unfortunately, we are majorly missing the mark with this perspective. We cannot exactly take our bank accounts with us when we die. Yet as infinite souls, we will be able to take pride in the joy we spread and the growth we achieve from the challenges we overcome.

It would be amazing if more of us could use our career to pursue our calling. We would see our quest for true inner alignment as more important than any college degree, parental expectation, or sparkly accolade we could receive in the outer world. We would realize that knowing ourselves and listening to our intuition is what will truly bring us the most success in the end. We would see what can help us make the greatest difference in a world that deeply needs us to stop hiding and start harnessing our talents and passions for the greater good of all, and we would make it happen by contributing our unique piece to the puzzle.

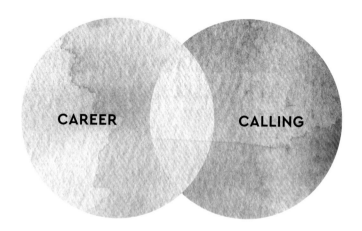

About Your Cosmic Guide to the Stars

I first started my journey with astrology because I was confused about my career, my relationship, my health, and who I even was. I thought I was following my heart, pursuing my dreams, and living my life to the fullest by doing what I loved, and I didn't understand why I still didn't feel fulfilled. I often felt like I was hiding who I really was, even from myself at times.

On paper, my life back then sounded like a dream come true. In 2015, I was running my own business as a graphic designer and working with dream clients all around the world. I had just become engaged, and my fiancé and I were able to buy our dream house in Hawaii. However, everything got flipped upside down when, within a month or two of moving into our home, a mysterious illness led me to have a terrifying near-death experience that sparked a spiritual awakening.

After coming back from that traumatic experience completely shaken, I set out to make the most out of my life and become the most authentic version of myself. There was so much more I still wanted to do and become. I suddenly understood just how sacred it was to even be alive. I couldn't keep wasting my time on earth doing anything that didn't light me up or that made me feel stuck or small.

The horoscopes I had been reading online while I went through this difficult time had resonated deeply, so I decided to dive deeper. I set out to gain a fuller understanding of astrology, myself, and my place in the universe so I could make the most of the life I was miraculously given back. Through learning how to read and decode my astrology chart, I discovered that I had been ignoring my intuition and living a life I *thought* would make me happy rather than honoring my inner knowing. Reading my chart helped clarify that and bring my authentic truth up to the surface to finally be confirmed and seen.

From my astrology chart, I found out that I was not meant to be doing the surface-level design work I had been doing. Instead, I was meant to help people on a deeper and more spiritual level. The design work was just meant to be one small aspect of my journey and not the whole path. Not wanting others to experience the fears I had around dying with my magic still inside of me, I finally had a clear mission. This mission fueled me to move forward and create a better future not only for myself but for all the people I could now help.

With the clarity and confidence that stemmed from having my calling laid out before me on a chart, and with my newfound knowledge of how to interpret it, I was able to make enormous life changes with relative ease. Within a matter of just a few months, I broke off my engagement, gave up my house, closed down my design business, and started an astrology practice from my parents' basement so I could help others transform their lives as well. I went from being shy and afraid of asking for what I wanted out of life to confidently owning my talents and gifts and using them to make a powerful impact on others, which also changed me for the better in the process.

Since 2016, I have been fortunate to help thousands of people tap into their cosmic calling, find their life's work, and give themselves permission to do what they really love, too. My clients and students have gone on to quit their limiting day jobs, create rewarding and impactful businesses, and start new passion projects and careers with which they can finally express their top talents in the way that feels most important to them for the highest good of their communities, themselves, and the world. This book is based on the soul discovery process I—and now many others—have gone through to transform my life and pursue my life's work. Now, it's time for me to pass this wisdom on to you. Let's get started!

How to Read Your Astrology Chart

To calculate your astrology chart, you will need to know the exact date, time, and location of your birth. With this information, a computer will be able to calculate where the planets and other major points were located in the map of the sky when you were born, which you will need to use as a guide as you go through this book.

Please note: If you are calculating a chart for another person, it is important to get their permission first. Reading someone's soul blueprint is considered deeply sacred, and this practice should be treated with care.

You can get your birth chart calculated for free online by entering your birth details at any of these sources:

✳ www.astroapp.com
✳ www.astro-charts.com
✳ www.astro.com (From the top menu, go to Free Horoscopes > Drawings & Calculations > Natal Chart, Ascendant)

You can also order a beautiful custom design of your birth chart on my website here: www.soulshineastrology.com/birthchart.

How Exact Does Your Birth Time Need to Be?

The chart shifts one degree every four minutes, so even if you are just an hour off, you could end up getting the wrong idea about yourself or someone else! That is why it's best to use a birth certificate or another written record to verify your details.

If you don't have your exact birth time, you can do an internet search for professional astrologers who offer rectification. Rectification is a service by which a skilled astrologer can start with what they know about your birth time (even if you can only tell them which day it falls on) and ask you a series of questions to correctly position where your planets would be in the sky in relation to your personality, behavior, and current life experiences. This will allow you to use this book safely knowing you have the correct birth time.

The main things to avoid reading on the chart if you don't have your exact birth time are the Moon Sign, Rising Sign, and Career Line. In addition to all the houses, these factors change rapidly hour by hour. Your Sun Sign and the other planets and points are still okay to read based on which zodiac sign they fall in, however, because they are not be likely to have changed much over the course of your day of birth.

The Basics of Chart Reading

Astrology charts are each presented a little bit differently when it comes to the design and colors, depending on where they are from. In Western Astrology, which is the type of astrology that is most commonly practiced in the mainstream today, astrology charts are circular. The chart is also referred to as a wheel.

Because this chart is used to track multiple cycles, you can think of the astrology wheel as a big three-dimensional clock that doesn't have a minute hand or second hand but instead shows different timelines of planets. Each planet moves at its own pace, with some going faster or slower than others as they orbit around the Sun. What you see on your chart is a snapshot of where the planets and other major points were located in the sky at the time of your birth from the vantage point of the exact location where you were born.

The idea is that when you are born into this world, you take on the qualities of that moment in time. Many astrologers also believe that we choose to be born at the exact moment that will be most advantageous for us in achieving our soul mission and learning our chosen soul lessons. That basically means that your birth information contains a secret code to unlocking your inner workings and getting one step closer to understanding your reason for being.

Let's start by breaking down the different sections on your chart.

Anatomy of an Astrology Chart

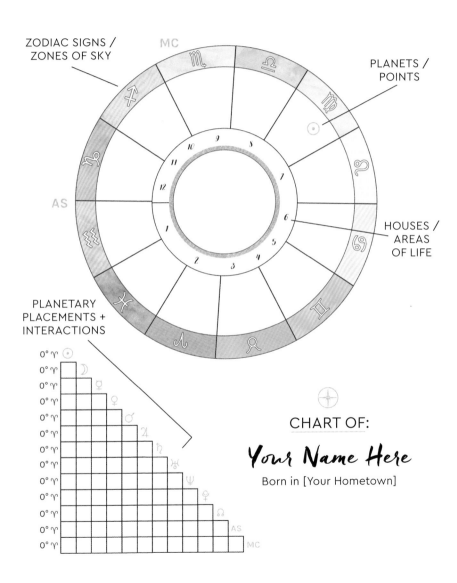

ZODIAC SIGNS /
ZONES OF SKY

MC

PLANETS /
POINTS

AS

HOUSES /
AREAS
OF LIFE

PLANETARY
PLACEMENTS +
INTERACTIONS

CHART OF:

Your Name Here

Born in [Your Hometown]

The Zodiac Signs

On the outermost rim of the astrology wheel, you'll see the twelve zodiac signs. These represent twelve different zones in the sky. Each zone of the sky—from Aries to Pisces—signifies a different set of characteristics or, in other words, a different mode of channeling our energy. Astrology is essentially the study of energy. We will be begin discussing the way each of the signs channels its energy in the next chapter.

At one time, these twelve zones of the sky may have correlated with the specific constellations they were initially named after. However, because the galaxy we live in is ever-expanding and growing, the constellations that we humans have tracked since the beginning of time have shifted. That is why Western Astrology is based on the journey the Earth takes to travel around the Sun.

When the Sun reaches the cardinal points in the sky, which are like cardinal directions, equinoxes and solstices occur. Each equinox and solstice signifies a shift of the Sun into one of the four cardinal signs of the zodiac, which are:

	Northern Hemisphere	Southern Hemisphere
Aries	Spring Equinox	Fall Equinox
Cancer	Summer Solstice	Winter Solstice
Libra	Fall Equinox	Spring Equinox
Capricorn	Winter Solstice	Summer Solstice

Degrees

Each zodiac sign—or zone of the sky—is broken down into thirty sub-sections marked with small notches. These are called degrees. The first degree of every sign is 0, and the last one is 29. You can think of degrees as being like those little lines on a ruler, explaining how far into the zodiac sign a planet or point on your chart is located.

Planets/Asteroids/Points

In the next layer of the astrology wheel going inward, you will find symbols that mark the planets and other points, such as asteroids, and even some mathematical calculations.

These are actually what we are tracking in order to discover more of who you are, what you care about most, and what you're here to do. The other areas of the chart simply provide the backdrop or, in other words, a way of understanding how that planet behaves based on the setting it's in.

When you read the chart out loud, start with the planet or point. For example, you would say, "My Sun is in Pisces in the 3rd House of Social Networking" or "My Neptune is in Capricorn in the 2nd House of Values, Desires, and Goal Setting."

Each planet, asteroid, or point reflects a different aspect of our energy. For example, Uranus represents our rebellious side, Mercury represents our interests, and Neptune describes what our ideal vision for the future is. You will learn all about the planets and other points and what they mean for you in Chapters 3 and 4.

The Houses

Heading inward another layer toward the middle of the wheel, you'll find twelve different-sized sections that contain numbers. Each section, referred to as a *house*, signifies one of twelve areas of life. This is where we begin to ground the universal energy and understand how it is most likely to materialize for us here on earth. The houses allow us to get even more specific so we can understand which area of our lives each planet or point's energy is being channeled into and whether that energy affects our relationships, health, family, career, or the like.

Planetary Mapping Worksheet

A great way to become more acquainted with your astrology chart is to write down which zodiac sign and house each of your planets, asteroids, and points falls in. To download a copy of this worksheet to record each of your planetary placements, go to www.soulshineastrology.com/book-resources. Alternatively, you can use a pencil to write them in the spaces provided opposite.

PLANETS		ZODIAC SIGN	HOUSE
☉	Sun		
☽	Moon		
AS	Ascendant		—
MC	Midheaven		—
☿	Mercury		
♀	Venus		
♂	Mars		
♃	Jupiter		
♄	Saturn		
♅	Uranus		
♆	Neptune		
♇	Pluto		
☊	North Node		
	South Node		
⚷	Chiron		
⚴	Pallas Athena		

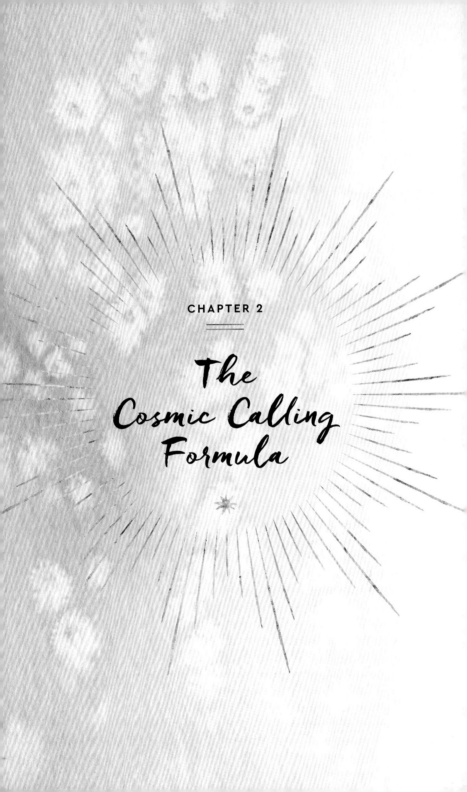

CHAPTER 2

The Cosmic Calling Formula

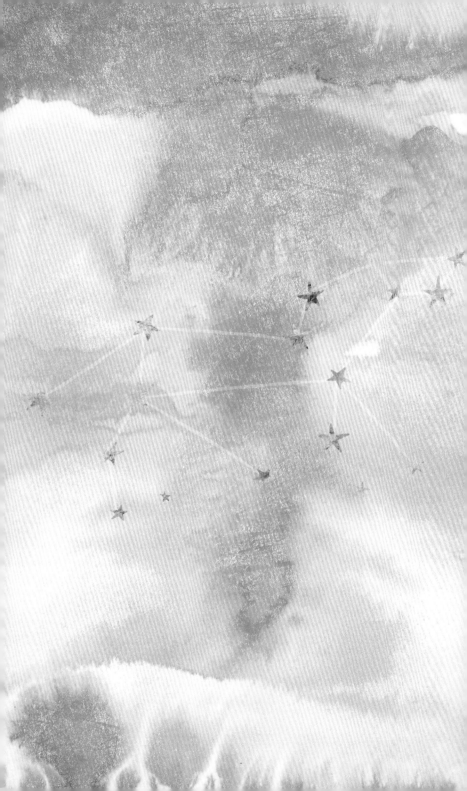

When people first learn they can use astrology to discover their calling in life, they often want to know which point to look at on their chart to uncover this information. The truth is, though, that there isn't one single symbol on your chart that can explain your whole personality or life path. Humans are too complex for that. Instead, it is important to take the entire astrology chart into consideration when you are using it to determine your soul's mission.

There is, however, a shortcut you can use to get an overview of who you are, and I call it the Cosmic Calling Formula. This formula covers the four main energetic signatures that explain your most basic instincts:

* **Your Sun Sign:** How you express yourself the best.
* **Your Moon Sign:** What makes you feel the happiest and the circumstances you need to feel fulfilled.
* **Your Rising Sign:** Your role and the work you are physically meant to do to be of service to others.
* **Your Career Line:** The desired outcome of your life's work and the legacy you are here to leave behind.

These four aspects of yourself are like the four cardinal directions of your life path or the crosshairs that allow you to zero in on the essence of who you are and what you are really here to do.

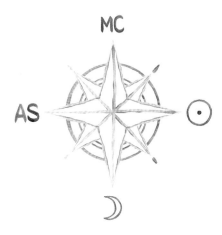

Sun Sign: Your Primary Essence

The Sun is your soul's primary essence. It is your life force, your *prana* or *qi*, your core personality, and the vital spark of energy that makes up your spirit. Think of the Sun in the sky and imagine how bright and intensely hot it is, with its rays of blinding light shining out and affecting everything else around it. Without the Sun, we would not have life. We would not even have astrology, because all the planets, points, and asteroids orbit around the Sun. It makes the plants—including our food—grow. Birds, bugs, and animals rely on it, and our ancestors even used to worship it.

One of the most important pieces of your entire astrology chart is your Sun Sign. It is determined based on where the Sun was in the sky on the day you were born, and you can find it by looking for the symbol that looks like a circle with a dot inside of it on your astrology chart. Most of us already know what our Sun Sign (or Star Sign) is, even if we haven't had the opportunity to learn that much about astrology yet, because it's what the horoscopes in magazines, on websites, and on astrology apps are based around. Although the Sun Sign is only one point on your astrology chart, it's where the majority of your life force energy is channeled, and it is what creates the essence of your personality and your perception of life.

When it comes to finding your calling, you will never be truly happy unless you are growing in the way *you* want to, according to your own desires and interests. This is something your Sun Sign can help you zoom into. A lot of us try to change ourselves to fit into situations that are not right for us, and then we blame ourselves when we don't "measure up." We can also be afraid to let our best qualities shine through due to fear, social conditioning, and limiting beliefs we have picked up that make us feel like we are not good enough. Your Sun Sign can help illuminate how you express yourself the best so you can honor your soul's unique expression and bring it out into the world with greater courage and confidence.

Did you know that the birthday date ranges for the zodiac signs that you read in newspapers and magazines aren't always accurate? Someone who is born on April 19 one year could be an Aries while someone else born on April 19 the following year could be a Taurus. This is because the Sun moves across the zodiac wheel a little more than one degree every day. From year to year, the sun seasons can actually change which date they line up with on the calendar. If you were born on a cusp—on the verge of another sign—make sure you are looking at your astrology chart to see which Sun Sign is yours.

ARIES

It makes sense that, as the first sign of the zodiac, Aries would strive to be the first to achieve something new. Known for being a pioneer as well as for being energetic, brave, assertive, spontaneous, and independent, an Aries is an individual through and through. They really don't like to be told what to do, so entrepreneurial ventures and leadership roles greatly appeal to them.

Aries express themselves best when they share what they are the most passionate about and encourage others to pursue their passions, too. They naturally pave the way simply by being who they are. They are here to take their enthusiasm for the things they love and spread it around like wildfire as they use their powerful influence to persuade others.

Quickly getting bored and impatient when there isn't a feeling of newness in their life, Aries also craves movement. They love to blaze new trails, which means they can even go too fast at times. They will want to choose a path where they can continuously be innovating, but ideally in a conscious manner where they are not leaving an endless stream of burnt down or half-baked ideas in their wake. Even if multi-passionate, as Aries are known to be, they may consider centering their personal brand around a few key themes that are closely related to what it is that makes them come alive most.

TAURUS

Taurus is the sensible and sensuous second sign of the zodiac. Deeply connected to the resources of the material plane, they are typically quite practical about the actions they take to achieve their aims. They can be good at getting things done steadily and efficiently when they have set their mind to accomplish something that is important to them.

Taurus is dependable. They tend to pursue their goals with a solid sense of determination to follow them through to the very end without letting anyone or anything change their mind. They make excellent business owners and managers because of their ability to create a firm foundation for future stability.

Taurus's deep appreciation for beauty, comfort, and stability provides them with the ability to help others feel more calm, supported, and serene. They like to move slowly and do not like to be rushed or bossed around. Instead, they want to be able to take their time and go at their own pace to create high quality things that will stand the test of time. Overall, it is important for Taurus to pursue projects that will allow them to feel the way they want to feel and that will also help others feel the way they want to feel.

GEMINI

Although it is the third sign of the zodiac, Gemini is known as the sign of the "twins" mainly because of how quickly they are known to change their minds. Constantly craving mental stimulation, Gemini gets easily bored when stuck doing the same thing in the same way or the same place every single day. Due to their insatiable craving for variety, Gemini needs a job where they can fill their day with many different people, activities, and learning opportunities to avoid becoming restless. Although they love being busy, they can take on too many things at once and get distracted. It's better for Gemini to do two vastly different things very well rather than ten that they never finish.

As the messenger of the zodiac, Gemini has a gift for explaining complicated information to others in a way that is easy for them to understand. Even just the simple tips and ideas they casually toss off in a conversation among friends have the power to change, improve, and simplify others' lives in important ways. It isn't even necessary to be the original source of this knowledge, as Gemini's role is simply to be a "re-source" and pass on what has interested and worked for them. Overall, Gemini's underlying drive is to make a statement or spread a message, and this is what they were born here to do.

CANCER

Cancer is best known for being empathetic, kind-hearted, and caring. Those born under this emotionally sensitive sign easily understand how others are feeling because they naturally pick up on the emotions of others around them. Often, the other person doesn't even need to say what they need out loud because Cancer will just know. This sign is mainly focused on nurturing and taking care of others, reflecting on their emotions, and creating a rich, stable personal life that will support them far into the future. They excel at making others feel comfortable, whether they are counseling, protecting, or caring for people in need. Sometimes, though, their deep level of concern for others can feel like a burden when they forget to put their own self-care first.

Safety, in general, is important to Cancer. They're not likely to take a risk unless they know for sure it is going to work out in their favor. Ideally, they can derive this sense of security by working with people they can get to know on a deeper level or by doing something they feel emotionally invested in. Above all, Cancer excels most when they can care for others in a way that makes those people feel seen, heard, and cared for as they look toward creating a more secure future for themselves in the process.

LEO

Leo craves to become the best and brightest at everything they do, and, as it turns out, they are naturally very good at a lot of things. As the rockstar of the zodiac, Leo loves to be recognized and appreciated for the unique gifts they bring to the world. Others will often look up to them as a shining example of what is possible. Anytime Leos seek to bring out the best in others, it will usually be well-received.

There are also Leos with an inferiority complex who are a bit shy and prefer not to be in the spotlight at all for fear of rejection. That is because what all Leos want most is to feel accepted so that they can share their generosity and love on full blast. These people need to remember it is still possible to become recognized as a master, expert, or top performer without needing to show off.

Overall, Leos are meant to do whatever brings them the most joy rather than caving to the demands and expectations of others. After all, it is their innate originality and childlike wonder that draws others to their work in the first place. When a Leo is excited about something, the people around them cannot help but be inspired by their confidence and love for having fun.

VIRGO

Virgos are often called upon to get things done efficiently. They have a keen ability to notice when something is off and can use their strong minds to figure out solutions to complex issues. They're also skilled with their hands and will typically prefer to do their work behind the scenes rather than be the one in front of the spotlight.

Virgos feel their best when they're being of service in practical ways that make life more sane or manageable for themselves and others. As natural healers and fixers, they are skilled at removing blocks or solving problems that are keeping others from moving forward. At the same time, they can easily get stuck in their own heads and can be overly self-critical when they aren't channeling their highly perceptive abilities in the right place.

A Virgo needs to feel like their life is organized, so setting up a schedule that supports them is an integral part of their ability to show up to do their best work for others. Ideally, they should be disciplined in adhering to a consistent ritual, routine, or schedule so they can feel well balanced. It is especially important for them to have periodic check-ins to look at the bigger picture of where they want all their hard work to be leading them.

LIBRA

As the middle sign of the zodiac, Libra is a purveyor of balance and harmony. Those born during this season can easily sense when others are unhappy, so they aim to please and try to spread good vibes wherever they go. Their creative talents and gift for language could make them a natural in any field in which a refined sense of artistic style is key.

Libra's natural charm wins others over easily, which is handy because, as the sign associated with relationships and partnerships, they can feel quite lost without another person to bounce their plentiful ideas off of. Despite their people-pleasing nature, however, Libras do prefer to be the ones in charge. They do their best work when they are leading the show, presenting concepts, and delegating their ideas for others to execute.

Overall, Libra expresses themselves best when they are supporting others in bringing more ease, flow, and alignment into their lives. Libra loves to bring people together to enjoy and appreciate the simple luxury of living life. If they truly enjoy and believe in what they do, they can be especially persuasive when it comes to sales because they can easily call on the right words to use to make others feel comfortable investing in them.

SCORPIO

If there is something a Scorpio wants, they will stop at nothing to make it happen. Despite their intense drive to further their own aims, Scorpio is also deeply skilled at understanding how others feel. They are empathetic, sensitive, and deeply sentimental, making it difficult for them to let go of the emotional shockwaves from events that happened long ago.

Ideally, a Scorpio should pursue a calling that allows them to go deep, as surface-level details will get very dull to them after a while. Scorpios need to feel connected to a line of work that holds greater meaning for them—perhaps even one that reflects some of the life challenges and lessons they have overcome. They also have a gift for transforming both people and materials, alchemizing them into new forms.

When it comes down to it, Scorpios are mostly concerned with getting to the core of the real issue behind people's problems. They are natural researchers and detectives who are not afraid to dig beneath the surface and look at things that others may find uncomfortable, difficult, or taboo. Scorpios tend to be good at managing other people but usually don't like being told what to do. Taking ownership over how they spend their time and earn their money is essential for a Scorpio because they yearn to feel like they have the maximum amount of power over their own lives.

SAGITTARIUS

Known for being spontaneous, optimistic, and enthusiastic, Sagittarius is always down for an adventure. They are incredibly adaptable to change; in fact, they crave it. A Sagittarius can become unhappy if they get stuck having to do the same thing the same way for too long, so it's common for them to jump around among many different jobs, projects, and ideas. Once they've mastered something, they are simply ready to move on to the next.

Sagittarius's greatest skills include envisioning new possibilities and encouraging others to see beyond the normal limits they put on reality. Their love of different cultures exposes them to many different philosophies and viewpoints, which grants them a sense of universal open-mindedness.

Freedom is incredibly important to a Sagittarius not only when it comes to going where they want to go but also in learning what they want to learn. They are lifelong students who love falling deep into a rabbit hole of research so they can truly understand their favorite subjects. Sagittarius is, however, the happiest when they can bring back what they have learned to share with others. That is why they make wonderful guides and mentors. They are here to draw on their vast experiences and interests to share about the many paths they have followed to develop greater wisdom.

CAPRICORN

It is not at all unusual for Capricorns to become high achievers due to the elevated standards they set for themselves. This sign is ambitious, responsible, resourceful, and sometimes quite strict or serious (especially with themselves). They have a strong need to plot things out in advance so they can avoid potential pitfalls and are likely to feel quite lost without a set schedule or plan.

A Capricorn's greatest superpower is their ability to structure and systemize the world around them. After they manage to create order for themselves, they pave the way for others to more easily reach their goals, too. For this reason, Capricorns make great teachers, coaches, bosses, CEOs, leaders, and business managers. Their persistence, resilience, and natural air of authority attract respect as they climb the ladder to greatness in whatever they choose to do.

Because Capricorn prefers to get things done as efficiently as possible, the thought of wasting time can be painful to them while, on the flip side, hard work and discipline can be quite therapeutic. They gain a lot of satisfaction from checking things off their to-do list, achieving their goals, and generally doing a job well done. It only makes sense that Capricorn would enjoy helping others get organized and on track with their goals, too.

AQUARIUS

Aquarius is the avant-garde sign that is here to bring us all into the future. An Aquarius loves to introduce new ideas and cutting-edge concepts that can help their colleagues, community, and society progress in much-needed ways. These are not the kind of people who like to follow the rules. Instead, Aquarius is all about challenging what is conventional and rebelling against the status quo. They prefer to do their own research rather than blindly follow what they're told.

Despite being an independent thinker, Aquarius appreciates the fact that they can achieve better results when working as a team. And although their greatest discoveries come from their radical daringness to be different, they do seek to find a sense of belonging among their peers. At the same time, Aquarius will still do their most important work alone. Their minds move quickly, and they don't want anyone or anything to hold them back or slow them down.

Those born during this season often feel like they are different from everyone else, but that is just because they are tuned into a frequency that others just aren't picking up on yet. They love to zoom ahead to understand the new wave of information that is coming in, but they truly express themselves best when they are sharing their time, talents, and resources to help equal the playing field for the people around them.

PISCES

Those born under this boundary-less sign live their lives partly in the realm of their own imagination. A Pisces is a natural healer because they easily sense how others are feeling, and their ability to envision vast and colorful landscapes within their mind makes them a whimsical creative artist. Although their high level of compassion can be overwhelming, it is when they come to realize their sensitivities are a gift and not a curse that they will finally step into their full superpowers.

Fueled by the desire to serve others in a purpose-driven way, Pisces express themselves best when encouraging others to seek out greater magic and meaning in their lives. However, it can be easy for them to shrink back and hide until they can find a way to serve that they can feel confident about. The trick for Pisces is not to get so obsessed with their fantasies that they don't bother to do the practical, physical work to make their dreams come true.

Overall, Pisces does their best work when they're in a comfortable environment where they feel safe to express who they are and how they really feel. Preferably working alone or surrounded by smaller groups of people who are understanding of their sensitive nature, they long to go deep to form an emotional bond both with their craft and with the people who benefit from it.

Sun in the Houses

You express yourself the best when you are...

Sun in the 1st House of Identity, Authenticity, and Leadership:
Asserting yourself as a leader by using your own personal story,
experiences, and challenges to fire others up.

Sun in the 2nd House of Values, Desires, and Goal Setting:
Encouraging others to achieve their desires or feel the way they
want to feel with careful consideration and smart planning.

Sun in the 3rd House of Social Networking:
Sharing ideas and messages that are conveyed in an easy-to-
understand way that connects people together.

Sun in the 4th House of Home, Family, and Long-term Security:
Taking care of your home and family, helping others improve theirs,
or holding space for others through your work.

Sun in the 5th House of Fun and Creativity:
Creating the fun, playful, artistic, or light-hearted things you
personally wish existed in the world in a bold and original way.

Sun in the 6th House of Health, Work, and Daily Rituals:
Helping others make their everyday life less stressful, unhealthy, or
chaotic by putting better systems, schedules, or routines in place.

Sun in the 7th House of Relationships and One-on-one Work:
Supporting others closely to help them bring a sense of beauty,
balance, peace, or harmony into their lives.

Sun in the 8th House of Business, Finance, and Shadow Work:
Bringing about an emotional, spiritual, or financial transformation or
breakthrough for others that elevates their perspective of life.

Sun in the 9th House of Education, Exploration, and Self-discovery:
Exploring the world and seeking out new information
and ideas in order to bring back what you learn to
help broaden the minds of others.

Sun in the 10th House of Career and Higher Calling:
Focusing your energy on leaving behind a meaningful, lasting legacy
that others can benefit from for years to come.

Sun in the 11th House of Friendship and Community Outreach:
Working on a team, in a group, or within your
community to bring about innovative changes that
will improve the lives of others around you.

Sun in the 12th House of Spirituality and Higher Purpose:
Seeking to align yourself with a greater soul mission
as well as connecting others with the insights and
inspiration they need to do the same.

Moon Sign: Your Emotional Needs

Feeling unfulfilled is usually the first sign you are not in alignment with your calling. Luckily, your Moon Sign can often help explain why. This point on your chart describes your emotional landscape and the circumstances you need to do your best work. It is also the side of you that you may try to hide when you are feeling vulnerable unless you are around someone who makes you feel safe.

Although the Moon in the sky may seem like it's simply a stunning spectacle to be witnessed on a clear, dark night, in astrology it is considered to be like a giant satellite that beams the frequency of the other planets' energy down here to us on Earth. Similarly to the effect it has on the ocean's tides, the Moon pulls on our emotions in different ways depending on its current phase and which zone of the sky it was in when we were born.

The Moon also explains what is in our comfort zone. Sometimes the best opportunities for growth lie beyond our comfort zone, but witnessing and honoring your Moon Sign can provide a nourishing resting place that can help you have a more enjoyable ride on this rollercoaster of life. We all have a particular set of basic needs and desires to meet in order to feel secure and happy in what we are spending our time doing. Understanding your Moon Sign, which is marked by the small crescent moon on your chart, will allow you to create the right conditions for you to feel your best and do your best work in a way that will be most fulfilling for you.

ARIES

Those born when the Moon was in Aries are quick to react and prefer to be very direct, whether they're happy or upset. They feel most fulfilled when life is moving forward at a fast pace and they can work independently and unhindered by other people's burdens or expectations. However, their impatience can sometimes lead them to squander opportunities that would have surely come in had they kept going longer and followed through.

When it comes to their work, Aries Moons love to activate and motivate others to pursue their passions. They have a lot of good ideas to share even if they don't have the time or energy to personally carry them all out themselves. Others around them greatly benefit from their inventive entrepreneurial spirit and willingness to take the reins and get new projects off the ground.

The ideal circumstance for an Aries Moon to thrive in would be one in which there is always a sense of newness or freshness involved in their projects. Whether this means always working with new people, promoting different products, or seeking to stay on the cutting edge, their work needs to keep them on their toes to keep their hearts full.

TAURUS

Taurus Moons desire to take their time and move at their own pace. This is a sign that loves to luxuriate in life and soak up every pleasure available in the moment. They don't see the need to rush because quality is more important than quantity to them any day. At the same time, Taurus Moons can be very stubborn. They dislike being told what to do, so working under an overly demanding boss or in a stressful, fast-paced setting would not be ideal.

With an innate drive to make themselves and others feel good, Taurus Moons may be drawn to work in the arts, with plants, in fashion, or even with food. They love helping people feel more serene, stable, and supported, and others are often drawn to their dependability and naturally calm and grounded demeanor.

To be most secure in their work, Taurus wants to feel like they're building something that will be sustainable, solid, and long-lasting. Because they're willing to work hard and put a great deal of time, patience, and consideration into anything they choose to do, they need to have solid, practical proof it will work out and be worth their time.

GEMINI

When the Moon is in Gemini, we tend to crave mental stimulation, so it makes sense that those born under this Moon Sign would naturally be restless when life seems to be moving too slowly. Gemini Moons don't do well sitting at a desk doing the same things the same way each day. They need to get up and talk to different people or to run around to different places to keep things interesting.

With quickly fluctuating moods in addition to their busy minds, Gemini Moons do not like being pinned down by their ideas. By the time the word gets out to others about how they feel, they may have already changed their tune. It's best for them to do work in which they can freely toss their ideas around without needing to take each one too seriously.

To feel most fulfilled in their work, this Moon Sign needs to be able to learn new things and share their thoughts, ideas, and favorite resources with others within a social environment. Rather than trying to do one thing at a time, Gemini Moons tend to get more done when multi-tasking. However, to avoid burning out, they should be careful not to make themselves busy with too many things.

CANCER

Intuitive, sympathetic, and deeply in tune with their emotions, Cancer Moons' feelings can sometimes be too much for them to handle, leading them to shut down or hide away in their homes. Cancer naturally longs to care for others because they easily notice when people are hurting, but they can also be prone to putting others' needs too far above their own.

Because of their sensitive nature, Cancer is a sign that is associated with seeking comfort and familiarity. Whether they're decorating their work cubicle, setting up the ultimate cozy home office, or creating a sacred space where they can meet with clients, Cancer Moons love to create a nurturing nest wherever they go. They're also happiest when working closely with people they can really get to know.

What a Cancer Moon needs to feel safe and fulfilled in their work is a foundation they know will support them. They tend to worry a lot when they're not sure what the future will hold, and they'll often stay stuck in jobs that they hate for fear of losing their security. If longing to fly free, they need to plan out a solid financial structure that is proven to be strategically aligned for success.

LEO

Leo Moons are creative and love to have fun. As natural leaders, they have an innate charm that inspires others while they seek to become the best at their craft. Passion is everything for them, and when they're excited about something, there is absolutely no limit to what they can achieve.

Although Leo Moons tend to be good at a lot of different things, they prefer to focus on one main project at a time. It can be hard for them to balance multiple tasks, deadlines, and timelines because they feel their best when they can focus on pouring all of their love into one main project that they feel the most passionate about pursuing. Leo Moons will know they've found their happy place when they're focusing on a task they can get lost in for hours on end.

Overall, Leo Moons need a creative outlet for their talents to shine through and a built-in opportunity to receive praise for their work. Because they put their whole heart into everything they do, it's understandable that they would become depressed in an environment in which they're not being recognized or appreciated for their talents or hard work.

VIRGO

Those born under a Virgo Moon are logical thinkers who often tend to bottle up their emotions. They don't like to seem weak or incompetent, so they'll typically avoid sharing how they feel. Although Virgo Moons are blessed with excellent critical thinking skills, they tend to over-analyze their personal problems and get stuck in their heads out of a yearning to find the perfect solution, which also happens to be one of their best skills when it is applied in the right environment.

To be most fulfilled, Virgo Moons need to feel like they're being of service to the world. Without a way to give back and help, they may feel drained, lost, or depressed. Whether they're caring for animals, healing or optimizing people's bodies, or meeting others' basic needs, their greatest joy is to be a helpful caretaker to society.

One of the main things that can throw Virgo Moons off their game when it comes to their work is being too self-critical. They can try so hard to avoid mistakes and attain an ideal of perfection that they don't take action on their creative downloads. With a love for making lists and a tendency to feel unsure of themselves without a plan, having a steady routine that supports them in their work, health, and overall wellbeing is ideal for their success.

LIBRA

Attuned to the beauty and harmony in the world, Libra Moons can easily tell when something is off. They're sensitive to their environment, so they often long to live in beautiful homes and work in nicely decorated offices that help them create a greater sense of balance for themselves. Skilled at picking up on others' feelings, Libra Moons can be especially prone to people-pleasing in their quest to bring about greater peace.

Because they can see both sides of every situation, Libra Moons sometimes get stuck going back and forth in their head. That's why it's best for them to work with a partner, a trusted mentor, or a friend they can call for back-up when they have a hard decision to make. Innately charming and gregarious, those born under this Moon Sign are also happiest helping other people to make them feel supported and light.

What Libra Moons need to feel most secure with their work is to surround themselves with people who respect and honor who they are and the ideas they have to share. When in the company of people who are dramatic or unreasonable, they should be careful not to inadvertently set their own needs aside to appease the crowd instead of taking a stand and doing what pleases them most in their work.

SCORPIO

Scorpio Moons feel their emotions on an intense level that not many of the other signs can comprehend. They crave depth and meaning as well as the ability to constantly evolve and transform. Work that is too surface-level or that doesn't allow room for growth is not likely to remain in a Scorpio Moon's life for very long.

This Moon Sign is happiest when they're researching a captivating topic or uncovering a problem's core issue. Scorpio Moons' minds are probing, constantly looking for answers and clues that others would not have the same level of persistence to search for, so any type of investigative work would appeal greatly to them.

To feel most secure, Scorpio Moons need to maintain a level of power and control over both their financial security and their emotional stability. They don't like being told what to do, so building their own business or doing work that allows them to choose their own hours or determine their own pay is ideal. They may also wish to work with a therapist, counselor, or coach in order to avoid falling into a negative mindset and getting in their own way.

SAGITTARIUS

Adaptable and usually unwilling to stay in a bad mood for long, Sagittarius Moons long to experience all that this world has to offer. They are curious individuals with a love of movement, change, and adventure. Those born under this Moon Sign seek to live a life of endless learning. They feel most fulfilled when they can share what has fascinated them the most with others.

Often hopping around to many different jobs due to their lust for new ideas and experiences, a Sagittarius Moon must always feel inspired by what they are learning, or they will disengage. Although they love to go deep to understand the subjects they find interesting, once they reach a level of mastery, they are ready to move on.

To feel stable and happy in their work, Sagittarius Moons should always strive to have something to look forward to. They need to follow what feels exciting to them in order to do their best work, give themselves permission to eventually step away from their projects, and move on to something new once they feel they've learned all they can.

CAPRICORN

Those born under a Capricorn Moon tend to take life rather seriously. They are driven and ambitious, and they must always have a goal and a plan to feel stable and in control. The greatest satisfaction for Capricorn Moons comes from getting things done right or simply knowing they are on track to getting where they want to be. One of the biggest lessons they're here to learn is how to let go and have fun.

Happiest when creating solid structures, systems, and programs to help others achieve their goals more efficiently and practically, Capricorn Moons feel a strong drive to live a productive life. They feel a lot of guilt if they can't do things perfectly or if they sense they've fallen behind, yet it's often only their own extremely high standards they're not meeting.

What a Capricorn Moon needs to feel most fulfilled in their work is the willingness and patience to break their goals down into smaller stages. They can achieve absolutely anything they put their minds to, but they need to learn to slow down and pace themselves to avoid freezing in place when they become overwhelmed.

AQUARIUS

Aquarius Moons live a life of the mind. Rather than getting entrapped by their emotions, they take a more logical and scientific stance to problem-solving. An Aquarius Moon makes a natural scientist, researcher, or journalist because they can produce an unbiased logical opinion without giving in to empathy or other outside influences.

Most fulfilled when discovering cutting-edge information and knowledge and spreading it on to others, Aquarius Moons do their best work on a computer, in a workshop or lab, or standing in front of a podium presenting their unique ideas. They long to make a meaningful difference in their community by solving the larger problems that are at play in the world and selflessly giving back.

Even though they're independent thinkers who love to work alone, it's important for Aquarius Moons to find a tribe of people who make them feel like they belong. Without friendships, a team, or a like-minded group with whom to share their ideas, Aquarius Moons will find that there is little fulfillment to be had and work can feel bland.

PISCES

Pisces Moons feel their emotions deeply. With a strong craving for exploring their creative and spiritual sides, they need to allow their strong intuition to guide their way. Pisces Moons love serving and helping others, and the extreme level of empathy they possess makes them natural mystics, talented healers, and patient listeners.

Because Pisces Moons soak up the emotions of others without trying, they may escape into films, books, art, music, or a meditation practice when the world around them feels too harsh. They naturally blend their ethereal energy with the people around them, which is why it's important for Pisces Moons to be discerning about the company they keep and the people with whom they choose to work. After even just a short period of socializing, they'll often need long stretches of time in their own world to unwind and recharge.

To feel most stable, safe, and fulfilled in their work, Pisces Moons need regular time to tap into their inner wisdom and imagination in healthy, supportive, or even artistic ways. Although they thrive when surrounded by positive role models who inspire them, they are happiest when they have an outlet for passing on their inspirations to uplift others.

Moon in the Houses

You feel the happiest and most fulfilled when you are...

Moon in the 1st House of Identity, Authenticity, and Leadership:
Being accepted and appreciated for being your true self as you step up as the leader of your own life.

Moon in the 2nd House of Values, Desires, and Goal Setting:
Focused on your goals and supporting and encouraging others to go after their goals in life.

Moon in the 3rd House of Social Networking:
Connecting people with new ideas and expressing what is on your mind in a variety of creative ways so you can't ever get bored.

**Moon in the 4th House of
Home, Family, and Long-term Security:**
Prioritizing your personal life over work and holding space for others to feel seen, heard, and cared for.

Moon in the 5th House of Fun and Creativity:
Expressing your creativity by inventing the things you wish existed in the world as well as helping others bring out their creativity.

Moon in the 6th House of Health, Work, and Daily Rituals:
Having consistent supportive rituals that keep you balanced as well as helping others adopt better habits, too.

Moon in the 7th House of Relationships and One-on-one Work:
Working with a partner or supporting another person
in making their life easier or better.

Moon in the 8th House of Business, Finance, and Shadow Work:
Diving deep beneath the surface to understand
a problem's core issue to bring about a major revelation,
reinvention, or transformation.

**Moon in the 9th House of
Education, Exploration, and Self-discovery:**
Seeking out new experiences that allow you to pursue
your curiosities and then bringing back what you have
learned to share with others.

Moon in the 10th House of Career and Higher Calling:
Creating a legacy that will further your
own status and sense of security in life while also
making a difference in many other people's lives.

Moon in the 11th House of Friendship and Community Outreach:
Giving back to your community and surrounding yourself with like-
minded people who make you feel like you belong.

Moon in the 12th House of Spirituality and Higher Purpose:
Aligning yourself with a greater vision that matters to you
on a soul level and helping others create a stronger
connection with their faith, intuition, or soul mission.

AS

Rising Sign: Your Identity and Your Role

The next most important aspect of the Cosmic Calling Formula is your Rising Sign, which describes your identity, the self you show to the world, and your role in society. The Rising Sign is also often referred to as the Ascendant, and you can find it on the left-hand side of your chart marked with an AS, ASC, or AC. This angle is based on where the sun was rising in the sky according to the angle of the horizon at the exact date, time, and location of your birth. It is often thought of as the initial impression that people get of you when you first meet.

This is one of the most important parts of your cosmic calling because it explains what you are meant to be physically doing as part of your life's work and the role you are here to provide for others, even though deep down you are so much more than whatever your job title or label is. You can also think of your Rising Sign as the mask or uniform you wear to do your job. Often, we will wear a mask to protect ourselves from being vulnerable because a lot of us are scared to share our true selves (our Sun Sign) with the world. In a way, the Rising Sign is like an outer shell of protection that keeps us safe.

Because the Ascendant rules over our identity and appearance, we even tend to look and dress like our Rising Sign. However, it can take some time to fully grow into. As we grow up, many of us will go through different phases with our personal style as we try to figure out who we really are. When you finally embody your Rising Sign, it is like finally coming home to yourself and stepping into the role of what you were always here to do and to become. It marks the very beginning of the 1st house, so in this case, you only need to read the zodiac sign.

ARIES RISING

The primary role of Aries Rising is to promote the things they're the most passionate about and to fire others up to take action. They crave movement, momentum, and advancement, which is why they make great coaches, accountability partners, artists, athletes, entrepreneurs, and innovators. Although they can sometimes be impulsive, overly direct, and impatient, a sense of passion is integral for Aries Rising's ideal role. Without it, they will feel flat, bored, and disconnected from their true selves. Aries also really love a good challenge! When it comes to pursuing their calling, their role is to constantly seek to improve themselves while pioneering new ideas and helping ignite others to create movement in their own lives.

TAURUS RISING

Taurus Rising is here to provide a sense of stability, calm, or serenity to others. Their role is to support the people around them by being a grounding influence in their lives. Often drawn to work that centers around practicality and sustainability, Taurus Rising is also skilled in the arts. Taurus Rising appreciates the creative nuances in a song, the subtle hints within a fragrance, and the sensual way brushstrokes flow across a page—all things that can make themself and others feel good. Some examples of job roles for Taurus Rising include artist, musician, designer, photographer, builder, banker, business owner, food industry worker, cosmetologist, fashion stylist, or gardener. Their love for luxuriating in life helps others slow down and get grounded in their bodies, too.

GEMINI RISING

As the messenger of the zodiac, Gemini Rising's role is to share ideas, resources, and tips that make life better for those around them. This sign has the cunning ability to explain complicated subjects in a way that meets others at their level of understanding by distilling the main takeaways. They're avid learners and they are made for any work involving writing, speaking, teaching, or visual communications. This Rising Sign also has a real gift for bringing people together to share interesting knowledge or to simply have a good time. Possible paths for Gemini Rising include being an entertainer, writer, social media influencer, party planner, PR agent, teacher, tech guru, or sales and marketing expert.

CANCER RISING

Cancer Rising's role is to nurture, protect, and comfort. They compassionately tend to the needs of others with both a sense of duty and a sense of joy. This Rising Sign is compelled to explore the distant past while helping others plan ahead to create a more stable foundation for their future. Some examples of possible job titles include counselor, caregiver, social worker, genealogist, nurse, police officer, EMT, financial planner, and human resource manager. Sometimes Cancer Rising worries about other people too much, so they will need to set strong boundaries if they choose to go into a line of work that could be emotionally straining. Because security and comfort are important to them, their main concern is making sure others know they will be fully safe in their care.

LEO RISING

A natural role model, Leo Rising is here to show others how they came to be where and who they are. Standing out as a shining example of what is possible for others, they seek to bring out the best in everyone they meet. This sign is generous with their creative talents and does their best work when it feels like play. Their childlike wonder could lead them into many different types of fields where they can easily rise to the top if they remain passionate about the process. The best paths for Leo Rising involve performing, presenting, training, managing, motivating, directing, or leading, as well as any role in which they can encourage others to become more creative and confident.

VIRGO RISING

Virgo Rising's role is to serve others in practical ways that make their everyday lives better, easier, more efficient, or more enjoyable. With excellent powers of observation, Virgo Rising does this by easily spotting and removing any blocks or barriers that have gotten in the way. They may be interested in writing, editing, accounting, administration, working with animals, or finding a career healing, improving, or adorning the body. Because they don't feel the need to be put in the spotlight, Virgo Rising is usually happy enough making sure things are ticking along for others while they work away in the background. Other possible job titles include project manager, healer, doctor, fashion designer, ritual leader, herbalist, and anything requiring a high level of craftsmanship, analysis, organization, or troubleshooting.

LIBRA RISING

The primary role of Libra Rising is to be a bringer of balance. Their job is to notice when things are off and make them feel right. Whether working with others one on one, creating designs, or decorating rooms, they bring a sense of charm, harmony, and flow wherever they go. Libra Rising is creative, good with words, and skilled at working in fields in which it's their job to make other people feel light and happy. Possible paths include beauty, language arts, design, styling, sales, customer service, acting, emceeing, politics, law, counseling, refereeing, or public service. Although they are self-starters and natural leaders, it may be best for Libra Rising to work with a partner or mentor because making decisions on their own can be hard.

SCORPIO RISING

A deep and perceptive thinker, Scorpio Rising is interested in uncovering the true core of an issue. Daring and sometimes intimidating, they are here to help others evolve to the next level and to facilitate a transformative process that allows others to see things from a new perspective. Potential paths for Scorpio Rising include method acting, art, detective work, therapy, finance, surgery, counseling, or being a healer, medium, mystic, or psychic. Whether they're alchemizing materials into new forms, doing investigative research, or helping others uncover the reasons behind their insecurities, they need a role that allows them to go beyond the superficial façade of everyday life and work to understand the true inner workings of their chosen subject and maximize their ability to create much-needed change.

SAGITTARIUS RISING

With a wanderlust for experiencing new things, Sagittarius Rising's role is to dive deeply into the subjects they are most interested in, inspired by, or curious about and then use what they've learned or experienced to bring guidance to others. Often introducing new ideas, concepts, and ways of life to all who benefit from their work, their job is to widen others' horizons of what is possible. Potential paths for Sagittarius Rising include teacher, mentor, tour guide, author, comedian, and any line of work that involves endless learning or travel. Freedom is important to them; they never like to feel stuck, so once they feel they have mastered a subject, they may quickly decide to move on to a new passion project that is piquing their curiosity next.

CAPRICORN RISING

Capricorn Rising makes a good coach, mentor, teacher, CEO, or boss. They are ambitious and well-organized, and they seek to live a proactive life based on achieving greater security or status for themselves so they can use their hard-working and often well-respected influence to help others. With a gift for creating efficient systems, structures, programs, and step-by-step paths, they make a natural authority figure who can help others accomplish their goals with precision, resourcefulness, and a high level of control. Capricorn Rising can thrive in chaotic situations where the pressure would be too much for other signs, but they need to be careful not to take on too much at once. Other possible paths for them include president, politician, sculptor, dentist, business manager, and any field in which they can methodically climb to the height of their version of success.

AQUARIUS RISING

The primary role of Aquarius Rising is to shake up the status quo. This sign naturally stands out from the crowd and seeks to bring new-age, forward-thinking, cutting-edge, or unconventional knowledge to the mainstream. Aquarius Rising is here to challenge the old ways of doing things and to bring a new world into being based on equality, humanitarianism, and a greater willingness to solve the problems that are prevalent in our communities. Potential paths for Aquarius Rising include activism, science, medicine, engineering, public media, politics, social work, teaching, and energy work. Whatever problems they put their mind toward solving, this sign's job is to help others bring about powerful changes that will allow them to break out of a rut, although their revelations may be surprising to others at first.

PISCES RISING

Dreamy and imaginative, Pisces Rising prefers to focus on the mystical side of life. Often living in daydreams and fantasies, this sign's role is to inspire and uplift others to believe in themselves and the magic of the world that may not always be seen or experienced in everyday life. They have a gift for helping others embrace more meaning in their lives through spirituality, creativity, or emotional support. Possible paths for Pisces Rising include healer, caretaker, nurse, artist, musician, and any form of work in which they can share their dream vision with the world. Although often introverted, they will quickly come out of their shell and exude confidence when they have an opportunity to serve others with their soul gifts.

Career Line:
Your Desired Impact

The final ingredient in the Cosmic Calling Formula is your Career Line. It's more commonly known as the Midheaven, and you can find it on your chart under "MC" which stands for *medum coeli* (Latin for "middle of the sky"). This angle on your chart denotes where the height of the sun would have been in the sky had it been fully risen at the moment and location of your birth. In other words, it expresses your highest possible potential for making a shining impact on others out in the world.

In addition to describing your public image, your Career Line (MC) helps explain the desired outcome for your life's work. It's your underlying drive for how you would like to make a difference, and it's the legacy that you want to leave behind or become known for. It's the way you do your work differently from others, and it's also how you ideally want to make other people feel. We often idolize people who have the same Sun Sign as our Career Line because we yearn to bring that type of energy out into the world, but often we already naturally do affect people in that way without even recognizing it.

The MC is also referred to as your Career Line because it always starts off the 10th house of Career and Higher Calling. Because this is the same stationary angle on everyone's charts, you only need to read the zodiac sign to discover what it means for you and the impact you are really here to create.

MC IN ARIES

Those with the sign of Aries falling in alignment with their Career Line want their work in the world to fire others up to take action. Often multi-passionate and multi-faceted in their interests, they seek to promote the things they feel most excited about in hopes that their enthusiasm will contagiously pass on to others. Most importantly, with a love for living a dynamic life filled with movement and acceleration, these people naturally inspire others to be independent, energetic, and more motivated to pursue their passions without worrying about what others will think. On the flip side, they typically don't like being told what to do because they want to figure things out for themselves as they seek out whatever brings them the greatest sensation of being alive.

MC IN TAURUS

People with Taurus on the Career Line hope that their work will allow others to feel more grounded, calm, and serene. They are supportive and dependable, and others often get the sense that they can be trusted. Taurus is also a sign that is about embodying and enjoying the pleasures of the material world. When there is something they want, they will be both persistent and patient, making sure they eventually get it. Overall, because Taurus is not a big fan of chaos or change, they focus on quality and sustainability, hoping that their work in the world will go on to provide a solid sense of stability for them and others.

MC IN GEMINI

The desired outcome of a Gemini Career Line's work is to inform, educate, entertain, and share ideas that may spark others to speak up and express their ideas freely, too. With a love of passing along tips and resources, people with a Gemini Career Line make helpful teachers even if not in the traditional sense. Often multi-passionate and interested in many different subjects, which can shift and change as quickly as the weather, they need a line of work that will stimulate their minds in a variety of compelling ways. Gemini loves to connect with people and will thrive most when they have an outlet or channel to transmit their musings out into the world.

MC IN CANCER

Those whose Career Line falls in Cancer aspire most to becoming a warm and compassionate source of comfort for others. Whether they feel compelled to protect the needs of those who are less advantaged or to provide a safe haven for others to process their emotions, their compassionate nature often draws in people who need healing, nurturing, or support. Home, family, and long-term security are also important concerns for Cancer, so helping others create a richer and more stable foundation for their personal lives may also come into play when it comes to the greater legacy they are working to create.

MC IN LEO

Someone with a Leo Career Line desires their work in the world to bring out the best and brightest in others. Simply by being who they are, they naturally inspire the people around them—including those they don't even know—to become more confident in sharing their creative self-expression. If they aspire to fame, it's mainly so they can show people what is possible when they harness their innate gifts and nurture their talents. Known for their high level of generosity, they hope to be appreciated and recognized for all that they share and give, but they need to be careful not to get a big head thinking they're the only one who knows best.

MC IN VIRGO

Those with Virgo on their Career Line are skilled at helping others identify what is holding them back. Whether they're doing manual labor, managing complex projects, or sharing their healing gifts, Virgo hopes to leave behind a legacy that will allow others to remove blocks or barriers to feeling more whole, in control, and in the flow with their desired daily lifestyle. At the same time, Virgo is not afraid to tell it like it is, so others will naturally come to them when they need a reality check. However, they may need to be careful about obsessing over perfectionism so much that they cut themselves off from their own organic creative process.

MC IN LIBRA

The desired outcome for a Libra Career Line is to bring a sense of beauty, balance, and harmony to the world around them. They can easily tell when someone or something is out of alignment, so the legacy they seek to leave behind is of smoothing over the rough edges in life and making others feel lighter. Possibly artistic with a flair for creative writing, Libra seeks to bring a flourish to everything they do in their work. Their naturally charming demeanor and ability to present their ideas confidently lifts others up and helps them breathe more beauty into life. True success for a Libra Career Line lies in supporting the success of others and increasing the level of peacefulness around them.

MC IN SCORPIO

Those with Scorpio as their Career Line are seeking to facilitate transformative work that has the power to completely change others' lives and the world. Skilled at getting to the core cause of an issue, they can root out what the real problem is and help others transcend it swiftly with their built-in psychological skills. Whether they're uncovering a hidden mystery, diving deep into other people's psyches, or transforming materials into new forms, Scorpio's incredible strength and powers of perception allow them to go into the deep crevices of existence that others would likely be too afraid to venture into. At the same time, they are always changing and transforming themselves, showing others it is safe and even empowering to shed what no longer serves to live a life of pursuing their true passions.

MC IN SAGITTARIUS

The legacy that someone with a Sagittarius Career Line
desires to leave behind is one of endless searching
for higher truths and inspiring others to believe in
greater possibilities. This is a dynamic sign that is always seeking to
learn and experience new things. Along their journey, they're likely
to learn quite a lot. When they bring back what they've learned to
help others see beyond the confines of their normal everyday lives,
they are fulfilled with the work they've done here on Earth. As natural
teachers and guides, a person with a Sagittarius Career Line hopes
to encourage others to feel more optimistic and expansive as they
zoom out to look at the bigger picture of life beyond what exists
inside their comfort zone.

MC IN CAPRICORN

People with a Career Line in Capricorn have a natural
air of authority that garners them respect. They are
confident and ambitious, and they can accomplish
anything they put their mind to so long as they don't try to take on
too much. Providing a system, structure, or program to help others
get on track with their goals also allows them to rise to a higher
level of status, security, and success. Their reputation is often very
important to them. They are willing to work hard to make a good
impression, and they can push their worries and insecurities aside
when needed to do so.

MC IN AQUARIUS

Spreading new-age, innovative, or cutting-edge knowledge to the masses is a big part of the legacy that those with an Aquarius Career Line are here to leave behind. With a strong desire to help society move forward, they can often be found in industries where there is a lot of innovation and change happening in the name of improving peoples' lives and the world. Although their eagerness to challenge the conventional may sometimes make others feel uncomfortable, Aquarius is meant to be different and to do things in their own unique way to spark charge.

MC IN PISCES

Those with Pisces on their Career Line naturally seek to inspire. They are empathetic and compassionate, and they love to live a life filled with imagination, idealism, and creative service. Although others may see them as passive, they simply need a lot more alone time than most to process their deeply felt emotions, which are left unprotected compared to the other signs. The legacy that Pisces Career Line people are here to leave behind is one of showing others that their intuition is their ultimate superpower. At the same time, they hope to help others believe in themselves and see the world as a magical place of healing, growth, and possibility the more they surrender and trust.

A Moment to Reflect

Now that you've learned the Cosmic Calling Formula, which covers the most important aspects of the chart and of your calling, things are about to get complicated. I invite you to take a moment to reflect on what you've read, how it relates to you and your past interests, and what you think your calling might be. From here on out, we are going to narrow down *how* to pursue that calling.

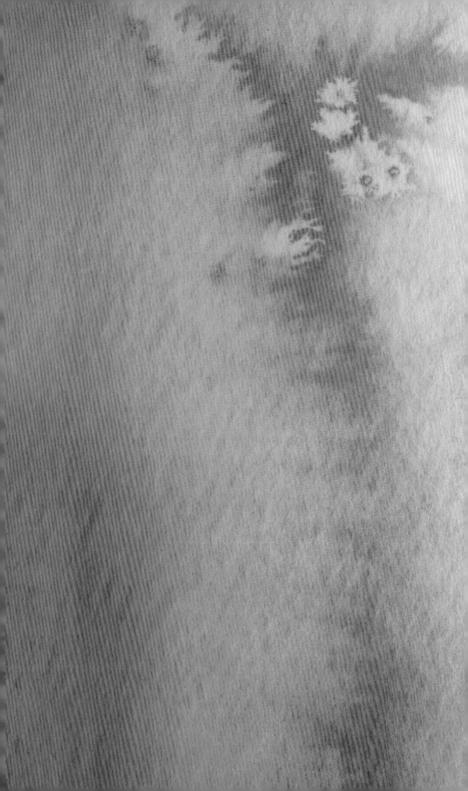

CHAPTER 3

The Planets
and Your Purpose

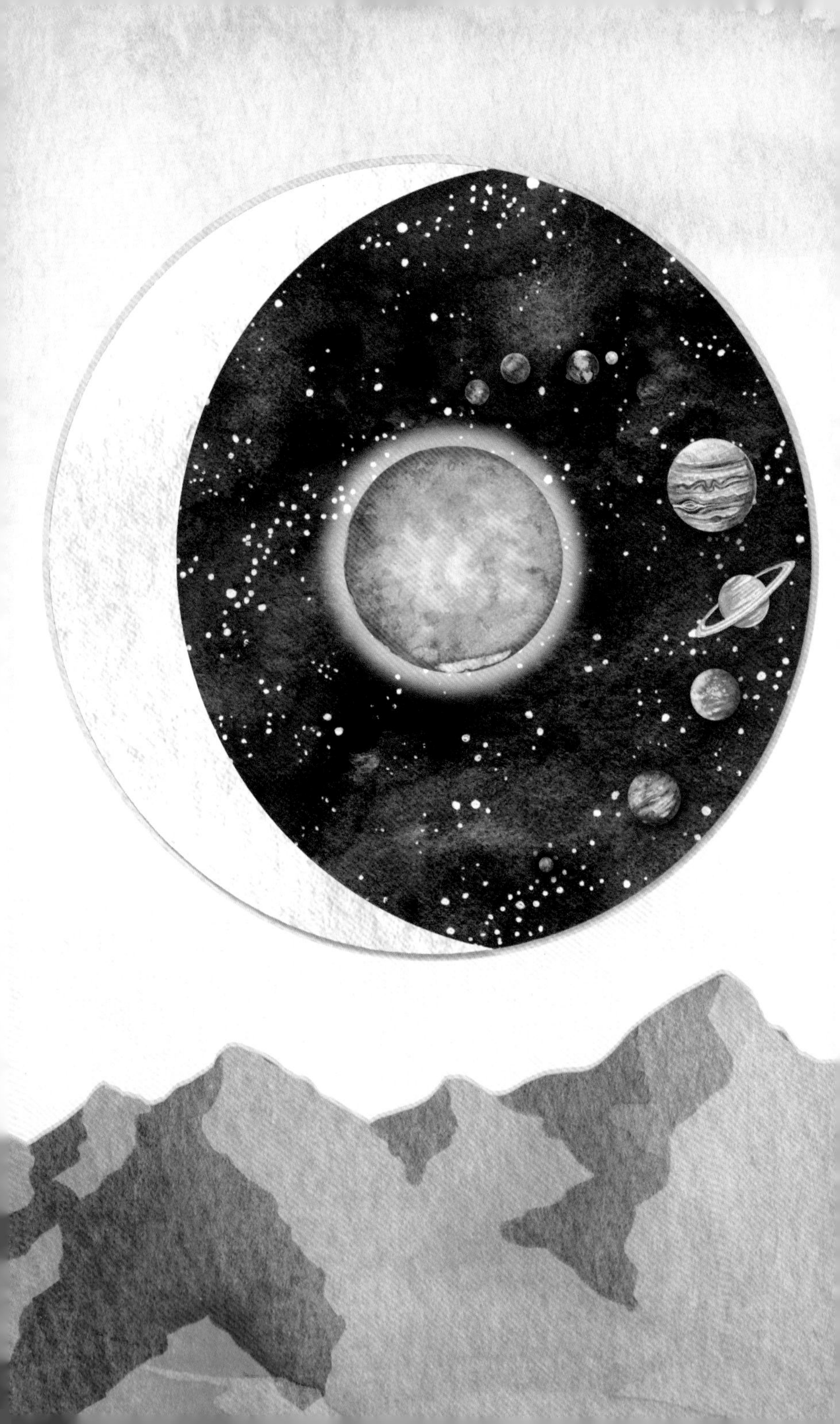

Since the dawn of time, our ancestors have looked up to the sky in search of answers, and they have tracked the planets to find them. Today, while astronomers talk about the planets of our solar system as being of a certain size, distance, or elemental composition, astrologers describe them with stories, myths, and archetypes that help us understand ourselves and our inner workings. This sacred wisdom, which has been passed down to present time, is so old that we don't have records of when humankind's work with the planets first began. Some records suggest it could go back as far as 8,000 years or more. All that modern-day astrologers know is that for whatever magical reason, these archetypes do resonate. The evidence and proof is right here in front of us in every facet of our daily lives.

When it comes to finding our purpose in life, the planets in the sky teach us that we are all wired to be a certain way. When we can work with our natural born circuitry, the positive energy flows. It's when we try to be someone we're not that we can twist our circuitry into knots and force ourselves to work much harder than we need to. When that happens, it can feel like we're swimming upstream or like we're going against the grain, and that's because we're challenging the cosmic order.

By venturing out further into the vastness of our solar system to plot out the planetary points on your astrology chart, you can discover how to harness your natural skills and talents to your advantage. In the following sections, search for where the symbols fall on your chart and use the zodiac sign and house descriptions to further clarify the specifics around your cosmic calling.

Retrograde planets: Every planet in the sky goes into retrograde at some point in its cycle. During this time, it appears to be moving backwards. When a planet is in retrograde, we become confused and unclear about how best to channel that planet's energy. It's unusual not to have at least one planet in retrograde on your chart because it happens so often. Those who have retrograde planets in their chart will see a little "r" or "Rx" next to the planetary symbol. On some charts, the symbol or degree number will simply be red.

In general, when a planet is in retrograde on your chart, you are more internally focused when channeling that planet's energy. You may be unclear about your intentions or direction as it relates to the energy that planet represents. Examples are provided in each of the following sections to help you interpret any retrograde (Rx) planets you may find on your chart in greater detail.

Mercury: Your Interests and Communication Style

The first planet from the Sun is Mercury. It rules over ideas, information, transportation, technology, schedules, and planning. On your astrology chart, the Mercury symbol, with two antennas on its head, explains what you like to think about, what you like to learn about, and the subjects you are interested in sharing. Mercury also symbolizes how your mind works and the ways in which you communicate best.

Mercury Retrograde: Mercury's frequently occurring retrograde cycle happens three or four times a year, the most of any planet. Those who were born during Mercury Retrograde may have trouble communicating their ideas clearly. Even if they think they know what they want to say in their head, it may not come out the way they had intended. That's why they often prefer writing to convey their ideas because they can take their time.

Soul Lesson: Those with Mercury Retrograde on their chart are here to learn how to hone their intuition and to come to trust in their own inner wisdom.

MERCURY IN ARIES

Mercury in Aries people are direct and to the point. This is an idea person with a sound entrepreneurial mind who does better in roles where they can give orders rather than be a follower. They are natural trendsetters who know what is going to be hip before anyone else and will need to have the freedom in their work to pursue their latest obsession wherever it leads.

Possible interests: personal and physical development, coaching, entrepreneurialism, new trends, fine art, performing art, martial art, athleticism, sports, fitness, fire, and personal defense.

MERCURY IN TAURUS

Those born with Mercury in Taurus tend to be quite set in their ways. Their mind is focused on creating stability and sustainability, which requires patience, and they have a lot of it unless someone tries to challenge their ideas. With a communication style that is slow and considered and a naturally calming voice, they like to take their time in expressing their ideas to make sure they can properly capture the essence.

Possible interests: business, finance, food, music, photography, fashion, film, fragrance, artful objects, manifestation, beauty, sensuality, gardening, nature, and cooking.

MERCURY IN GEMINI

With Mercury in Gemini, the mind is carried in many different directions and toward a variety of interests. This is a sign that loves to learn and share ideas, but they also get bored easily. That's why producing smaller blurbs of content will be easier for them than trying to keep their mind focused on writing something as long as a whole book. Ideally, they need an outlet with which they transmit their thoughts freely without being nailed down to any one topic.

Possible interests: technology, publishing, podcasting, journalism, blogs, social media, networking, party planning, games, trivia, and comedy.

MERCURY IN CANCER

Those who have Mercury in Cancer come across to others as being caring and gentle. Their mind is deeply attuned toward the feelings of others, which makes them want to use their words to nurture and support. They are especially good listeners. People are often drawn to Mercury in Cancer's work because of their compassion and ability to reflect and mirror back what the other person needs to hear.

Possible interests: women and children, social work, human rights, genealogy, ancestral healing, financial planning, cooking, home building or decoration, and being near water.

MERCURY IN LEO

Mercury in Leo people long to be heard and valued for their ideas. They communicate best when showing others how to stand up more confidently for their creative ideas or sharing how they do the things they've done. Instead of multi-tasking, they prefer to concentrate their energy on one central project at a time. It may even be hard for them to pull themselves away from something once their initial interest has been piqued.

Possible interests: art, photography, fitness, sports, working with children, leadership, coaching, shopping, singing, dance, drama, and writing.

MERCURY IN VIRGO

Those born with Mercury in Virgo have a focused mind that notices every detail, but they need to make sure they regularly take time to zoom out and see the bigger picture to ensure they are focusing on the right things. They can be very self-critical because they are constantly looking for things to improve, so it's best to do work that will put this skill to good use. Because they're so analytical, they generally avoid discussing their feelings.

Possible interests: accounting, animals, health and healing, nature, ritual work, herbalism, gardening, construction, science, technology, medicine, writing, and working with their hands.

MERCURY IN LIBRA

Those born with Mercury in Libra have a flair for using both their words and their writing to charm and uplift others. Because they desire to bring beauty and harmony into the world by sharing their ideas, they can easily notice when other people or things are not in balance. They think best when they can describe their ideas to another person so they don't get too caught up in their own heads.

Possible interests: beauty, art, architecture, design, fashion, yoga, relationships, politics, law, creative writing, channeling, and emceeing.

MERCURY IN SCORPIO

Mercury in Scorpio has a probing mind that is capable of diving to great depths to understand complex people and issues. Although they are secretive about their own worries, they fearlessly and curiously seek to understand the source of others' issues and insecurities. Most of all, they are captivated by the idea of finding solutions that create a powerful change or transformation.

Possible interests: psychoanalysis, research or detective work, real estate, business, finance, investing, spirituality, shadow work, energy healing, death, sexual empowerment, and hypnosis.

MERCURY IN SAGITTARIUS

Those born when Mercury was in Sagittarius are optimistic, intellectual, and witty. Their endless love of learning sends them out in search of new experiences and adventures as they aim to make sense of the world. As big-picture thinkers, they are not always as skilled at paying attention to the smaller details. However, it is their inspiring philosophy and expansive perspective that ultimately draws others to want to learn about their teachings.

Possible interests: travel, teaching, education, books, courses, spirituality, religion, foreign cultures, and animals (especially horses).

MERCURY IN CAPRICORN

Mercury in Capricorn is concerned with achievement, productivity, and not wasting words. Their minds are serious and focused on optimizing their output as they attempt to meet their own incredibly high standards, often beating up on themselves when they inevitably fall short. However, because of their persistence and strong ambition, this sign can figure out the solution to any problem they set their mind to. The trick is to focus on the right ones.

Possible interests: business development, organization, administration, planning, coaching, teaching, corporate work, construction, mending bones, crisis response, and mentorship.

MERCURY IN AQUARIUS

Mercury in Aquarius is forward-thinking and intrigued by new-age and cutting-edge information. Their mind can understand complex progressive concepts, and they can find innovative solutions to solve widespread problems in their community. Although they feel compelled to try to fit in with the group, their individualistic and often rebellious nature can't help but make them stand out as they share genius insights that shake up others' views of the world.

Possible interests: new-age wisdom, energy work, astrology, astronomy, aviation, science, technology, education, medicine, public media, activism, communications, and charity work.

MERCURY IN PISCES

Those born with Mercury in Pisces have a scattered mind that can make it hard for them to plan. Because they receive their best insights from tapping into their imagination, emotions, and dreams, they work best when solving problems that are soul-deep rather than logical and scientific. This sign easily picks up on how others are feeling and seeks to share ideas that inspire those around them to dream bigger and believe in themselves more.

Possible interests: dream work, psychology, mindset work, meditation, crystals, art, film, music, Reiki, and spiritual healing.

Mercury in the Houses

You enjoy sharing your ideas the most when...

Mercury in the 1st House of
Identity, Authenticity, and Leadership:

Standing up as a leader, sharing your story and journey, and showing others how you achieved success or overcame an obstacle.

Mercury in the 2nd House of Values, Desires, and Goal Setting:

Encouraging others to go after what they want and believe in their ability to achieve their true desires.

Mercury in the 3rd House of Social Networking:

Collaborating and connecting with like-minded people while jumping around to a variety of different subjects.

Mercury in the 4th House of
Home, Family, and Long-term Security:

Helping others in need feel safe, comforted, and cared for.

Mercury in the 5th House of Fun and Creativity:

Inventing the things you wish existed in the world in a fun, original, and creative way that brings inspiration to others.

Mercury in the 6th House of Health, Work, and Daily Rituals:

Serving others to make their everyday life easier, better, or more efficient while removing blocks or barriers that may get in the way.

Mercury in the 7th House of Relationships and One-on-one Work:
Supporting others as an assistant, partner,
or mentor in a one-on-one setting.

**Mercury in the 8th House of
Business, Finance, and Shadow Work:**
Uncovering the true core of an issue and digging deep to
research the most strategic way to solve or transcend it.

**Mercury in the 9th House of
Education, Exploration, and Self-discovery:**
Endlessly seeking knowledge and interesting life experiences and
bringing back your insights and findings to help guide others.

Mercury in the 10th House of Career and Higher Calling:
Combining your natural talents and interests to impact the world in a
positive way and gaining recognition for it.

**Mercury in the 11th House of
Friendship and Community Outreach:**
Helping to solve problems for your community to improve society
and bring people together around a common cause.

Mercury in the 12th House of Spirituality and Higher Purpose:
Revealing hidden truths, healing others, or aligning
your energy with a higher purpose or greater meaning
that feels important to your soul.

Venus: Your Values and Desires

Venus is the planet associated with femininity and our ability to open our hearts to receive our desires. Regardless of your gender identity, this planetary symbol, with the small plus sign under a circle, explains what you value most and the qualities that add to your experience of life. As members of the human race, we have common values including love, money, and beauty. We also have our own set of values and people we're drawn to because they help us live in harmony with how we want to feel as individuals.

Venus Retrograde: Because it only happens once every eighteen months for about six weeks, it would be somewhat more unusual to have Venus in retrograde on your chart. Those born during this phase may have difficulty expressing their desires or putting what is most pleasurable to them into a prioritized order. Because there is often confusion around love and money matters, they must experiment to find what feels best and be willing to reflect on their mistakes until they find their way.

Soul Lesson: If you have Venus Retrograde on your chart, you are here to learn about valuing yourself and believing in your own inherent worth instead of giving your power over to other people, money, or material things.

VENUS IN ARIES

Those born with Venus in Aries want to live a life that feels exciting and dynamic. They won't take no for an answer. Instead, it's an invitation to try harder to prove themselves. When it comes to love, they fall fast. Money often goes out as quickly as it comes in for them because they value speed, movement, and being the first to try something new. Drawn to fast-paced fields in which each day is different, their impatient nature will often see them jumping to something new once the freshness of a project wears off.

They work best with people who are self-starters, risk-takers, fast thinkers, entrepreneurial, athletic, active, independent, proactive, passionate, daring, brave, and direct.

VENUS IN TAURUS

With Venus in Taurus, we find someone whose main desire is to feel good and to make others around them feel good. With a preference for things that are made with a high degree of quality and care, they may become quite attached to collecting material things. Most importantly, this is not a sign that likes to be rushed. They prefer slow, steady action that eventually leads them to a stable sense of success and to be surrounded by pleasure and beauty.

They work best with people who are respectful, dependable, responsible, determined, persistent, supportive, tolerant, tasteful, and patient.

VENUS IN GEMINI

As someone with quickly fluctuating tastes, Venus in Gemini often changes their mind about what they want. They like to keep busy with a variety of different people, places, and interests, so they'll often avoid trying to get pinned down to any particular goal. Whatever the subject they're into at the time, this sign loves to talk, share, and socialize in a free-flowing manner. Making their money from being an informative resource for others would be ideal.

They work best with people who are witty, light-hearted, logical, fast-moving, talkative, easy-going, discerning, and socially aware.

VENUS IN CANCER

Venus in Cancer craves a strong emotional connection with their work. They care deeply for those in need, but they must set clear boundaries to avoid getting overly sucked into other peoples' drama. It's important for this sign to feel like they will be safe and supported far into the future, which is why they often seek out fields with a steady paycheck involved. When it comes to coworkers, they like to surround themselves with people with whom they can form long-term relationships and cultivate the feeling of having a second family.

They work best with people who are caring, compassionate, understanding, protective, loyal, conscientious, and kind-hearted.

VENUS IN LEO

Those born with Venus in Leo desire to be seen, heard, and recognized for their creative gifts. They generously give to others, which can sometimes make them prone to overspending. When they find something (or someone) they love, they can't help but want to pour their whole heart into it. Most of all, Venus in Leo people want to find something they can become the best at and focus all their attention on improving their skills until they do.

They work best with people who are confident, creative, outspoken, affectionate, giving, inspiring, and fun.

VENUS IN VIRGO

There is nothing more satisfying in their work to Venus in Virgo than managing to achieve an acceptable level of perfectionism. However, they can be their own worst enemy when cutting down their own creative ideas. What Venus in Virgo values most is being able to serve others by finding a consistent process in which they can get blissfully lost. With a love for planning and crafting the perfect routine or ritual, they feel best when they are prioritizing their time around supporting their joy.

They work best with people who are punctual, analytical, logical, grounded, efficient, minimalistic, and practical.

VENUS IN LIBRA

As someone with an elevated sense of style and taste, Venus in Libra is drawn to the lovelier side of life. Along with their deep appreciation for beauty and harmony, they are sensitive to the people and things in their environment and may feel bothered when things are not refined or in balance. Venus in Libra is also a total people person who loves to socialize and tries to make others feel good wherever they go.

They work best with people who are charming, gracious, accommodating, professional, kind, perceptive, and light-hearted.

VENUS IN SCORPIO

Venus in Scorpio longs to dive deep and understand the inner workings of the people and things around them. They make intense lovers and strategic businesspeople because they take the things they value very seriously. They are lured in by the idea of transformation, renewal, and rebirth, so they need to be able to continually evolve in whatever they choose to do.

They work best with people who are loyal, brave, observant, intimidating, mysterious, passionate, powerful, deep, and determined.

VENUS IN SAGITTARIUS

Those born with Venus in Sagittarius greatly value their freedom. As visionaries and freethinkers, they long to live life as if it were one big adventure with endless avenues for growth and expansion. This sign does not like to be stuck doing the same things every day, and they need lots of unscheduled space to follow their curiosities. When they can use the knowledge that they've picked up to guide others, they will feel fulfilled and complete.

They work best with people who are open-minded, adventurous, spontaneous, energetic, fast-moving, imaginative, and optimistic.

VENUS IN CAPRICORN

For Venus in Capricorn, it's good old-fashioned conventional values that make their heart flutter. Drawn toward the desire to create a stable and secure financial foundation for their future, they will only truly feel fulfilled if they attain it by using their talents to help support others. This sign seeks satisfaction through productivity and getting things done as they work to climb the ladder to the highest height of their own imagined version of success.

They work best with people who are ambitious, resourceful, proactive, authoritative, educated, experienced, and driven.

VENUS IN AQUARIUS

Venus in Aquarius values their community and wants to do their part to make the world a better place. With a love of anything unique, different, cutting-edge, or weird, they are often drawn to explore interests that are far from mainstream. This sign takes extra pleasure when they can make their money by innovating or inventing something new.

They work best with people who are eccentric, inventive, radical, rebellious, logical, conscientious, open-minded, and visionary.

VENUS IN PISCES

For those born with Venus in Pisces, being able to flow through life at their own pace, and getting creatively inspired along the way, is their idea of heaven. Often getting lost in daydreams and fantasies, these are creative people who feel their best when they can bring the visions of their imagination to life. They are natural healers and counselors because their empathic nature allows them to sense intuitively what others need.

They work best with people who are imaginative, insightful, creative, artistic, inspiring, uplifting, caring, and compassionate.

Venus in the Houses

Your greatest values in life revolve around...

Venus in the 1st House of
Identity, Authenticity, and Leadership:
Keeping up your appearance, looking and feeling good in your body, and inspiring others with your magnetizing presence.

Venus in the 2nd House of Values, Desires, and Goal Setting:
Improving your self-worth, believing you can achieve your dreams, and encouraging others to go after what they want.

Venus in the 3rd House of Social Networking:
Surrounding yourself with interesting people and ideas, sharing about the things you love, and connecting others.

Venus in the 4th House of Home, Family, and Long-term Security:
Creating a rich personal life that nourishes you and your family as well as holding space for others to feel seen, heard, and cared for.

Venus in the 5th House of Fun and Creativity:
Expressing your creative and original ideas, having fun, working with children, and devising new inventions that fulfill your own desires.

Venus in the 6th House of Health, Work, and Daily Rituals:
Keeping your everyday life and work balanced while prioritizing your days based on what will support you most.

Venus in the 7th House of Relationships and One-on-one Work:
Making other people feel supported in dealing with their problems
and creating closer connections with the ones you love.

**Venus in the 8th House of
Business, Finance, and Shadow Work:**
Being in control of your own time and money and stepping past
fearful beliefs to claim your sovereignty.

**Venus in the 9th House of
Education, Exploration, and Self-discovery:**
Seeking a deeper understanding of the world and using your
experiences to pass guidance on to others.

Venus in the 10th House of Career and Higher Calling:
Making a powerful impact through your career by harnessing your
natural talents, interests, and skills to your advantage.

**Venus in the 11th House of
Friendship and Community Outreach:**
Reaching out to help your friends and community in a unique way
that helps them feel supported.

Venus in the 12th House of Spirituality and Higher Purpose:
Aligning yourself with a greater mission that feels deeply
important to you on a soul level.

Mars: Your Motivation and Drive

Mars is associated with masculinity and our drive to reach out and grab the things we want in life. Regardless of your gender identity, this planetary symbol on your chart, with its arrow rising up to the right side over a circle, explains what motivates and inspires you to work hard and take action toward your goals. When we feel dispassionate and unmotivated, it's often because we're focusing on the wrong activities. When you're not aligned with your passions, it can feel impossible to get anything done. When you know your Mars Sign and House, you can focus your attention on more of the activities that fuel you to go out and conquer your surroundings.

Mars Retrograde: Those born during Mars Retrograde, which occurs only once every two years or so and lasts for about ten weeks, may have trouble understanding what motivates them. They work best when they allow themselves to let whatever feels most exciting that day be where they put their focus instead of trying to plan out their moves in advance.

Soul Lesson: Slow down and carefully consider how you are channeling your energy in the moment instead of mindlessly pushing things forward solely for momentum's sake. Follow your own intuition more when it comes to pursuing your goals.

MARS IN ARIES

Someone with Mars in Aries needs to act on their inspirations as soon as possible. If they spend too much time thinking about something they want to do, their desire to make it happen will quickly wear off. At the same time, it's not wise to be so impulsive that they don't stop to think things through. They should learn to expect that they will always want to keep moving and growing and give themselves the freedom to pursue whatever feels fresh, exciting, and new.

MARS IN TAURUS

There is nothing more important for Mars in Taurus than being able to take their time to do quality work. If they are rushed and unable to execute a project to their high standards, it takes all the pleasure away from their creative process. At the same time, they don't like to give up on what they've started. This sign is looking for a subject they can continue to stay committed to far into the future. When choosing a new career path or a major in college, they will take their time to make sure they are making the most sustainable choice.

MARS IN GEMINI

Those who have Mars in Gemini feel the most motivated when they can keep their mind stimulated with many different subjects. They need an outlet to express themselves and a willing audience that is happy to listen to their ideas. They love to keep themselves busy. In fact, they do their best work when multi-tasking, as long as they only try to balance a few things at a time. Being able to collaborate and bounce ideas off others also gets them excited to move forward and be productive.

MARS IN CANCER

Creating a firm foundation for their future is what gets Mars in Cancer out of bed in the morning. A craving for comfort, security, and control over where they are heading will point them toward seeking work that promises a big pay-off. They do their best work when caring for those who need their help, as that can be just as rewarding as money. They will be motivated if they have an emotional connection to their craft and feel that it supports them in return.

MARS IN LEO

Mars in Leo people are driven to become the best at what they choose to do. Competitive, brave, and daring, they prefer to do work that will offer them a chance to stand out and be recognized for their hard work and talents. This sign feels fired up when they can create the things that they wish existed and to do work that feels playful and fun. When they're not being appreciated or noticed for their efforts, they may find that their heart is no longer in their work.

MARS IN VIRGO

Someone with Mars in Virgo always needs to have a plan. Without an ordered list of their priorities and a schedule, they won't have the certainty they need to get a new idea off the ground. Mars in Virgo is most motivated when they can use their high level of perception to positively serve others. They will feel compelled to work hard when they feel that attaining a level of perfection in their chosen craft is actually in their reach by breaking it down into smaller steps.

MARS IN LIBRA

Those who have Mars in Libra are motivated by pleasing other people. If there's something they need to get done, their best bet is to ask someone to hold them accountable. Without a trusted partner, friend, or mentor to help them clarify their ideas and make decisions on their plans, they will often stay stuck in their own head. Because they are such a people person, Mars in Libra will want to work the hardest when they are supporting others in a way that also makes them feel good.

MARS IN SCORPIO

Mars in Scorpio needs to have a deep level of emotional connection to their work. Due to their intense drive for growth and transformation, they will stop at almost nothing when there is a specific goal they want to accomplish. Whether they are seeking a greater sense of financial success or emotional stability, this sign is motivated by the tantalizing quest to start from the bottom and end up on top. They will want to work the hardest in a field where there is always something interesting to figure out with a potential reward on the other side.

MARS IN SAGITTARIUS

Mars in Sagittarius is motivated by the opportunity for growth and expansion. When stuck in a field that doesn't interest them, they will procrastinate mercilessly. Interestingly enough, the things they stay up late looking at on the internet just for fun or to pass the time are often what they would excel at making part of their job. While they often don't like to follow the advice of others, they feel most energized when they can gather bits of all they've learned to provide guidance, training, or support to another.

MARS IN CAPRICORN

Mars in Capricorn has a strong innate drive to succeed and achieve. This sign feels most motivated when they've laid out a grand master plan to achieve their next big life or work milestone. They love to challenge themselves to undergo a lot of pressure and meet a high standard even though they may come to resent the immensity of their ambition later. Mars in Capricorn wants to work the hardest when they can devise a system, program, or path other people can follow to efficiently and resourcefully achieve a worthy goal.

MARS IN AQUARIUS

Those who have Mars in Aquarius are fueled by the desire to make a difference that helps improve the lives of others in their community. Without a cause to stand up for or something interesting to research, they won't feel inspired to work very hard. Because they often march along to the beat of their own drum, they feel unmotivated when forced to do things in a specific way that has been set out for them by someone else. They do their best work when breaking the rules, shaking up the system, and encouraging others to try a new approach to reaching their goals.

MARS IN PISCES

Mars in Pisces people need to feel creatively inspired. They have vivid imaginations and a strong drive to bring greater meaning, magic, and healing to their lives and to the world. One of the more artistic signs, they don't like to get nailed down to a system, schedule, or a set way of doing things. Instead, Mars in Pisces thrives when they have the freedom to follow what feels good and use what they love to serve others.

Mars in the Houses

You feel the most motivated when...

Mars in the 1st House of Identity, Authenticity, and Leadership:
Taking a stand for something that is important to you, pioneering a new idea, or standing up as an inspirational figure.

Mars in the 2nd House of Values, Desires, and Goal Setting:
Planning how to achieve your goals or helping encourage others to work toward what they want.

Mars in the 3rd House of Social Networking:
Connecting like-minded people with new ideas and sharing information in a way that is easily accessible to others.

**Mars in the 4th House of
Home, Family, and Long-term Security:**
Creating a firm sense of security for your future while focusing on developing a rich personal, family, and home life outside of work.

Mars in the 5th House of Fun and Creativity:
Creating the things you personally wish existed in the world and having lots of free time to have fun.

Mars in the 6th House of Health, Work, and Daily Rituals:
Setting up consistent routines and supportive habits that allow you to feel your best and do your best work for others.

Mars in the 7th House of Relationships and One-on-one Work:
Encouraging and supporting others to go after their passions and make progress on their goals.

Mars in the 8th House of Business, Finance, and Shadow Work:
Earning your own money and spending your time on your own terms while also helping others tap into their own innate power.

**Mars in the 9th House of
Education, Exploration, and Self-discovery:**
Diving deep to explore your own interests and fascinations and then bringing back what you've learned to guide and teach others.

Mars in the 10th House of Career and Higher Calling:
Harnessing your natural talents and fascinations to create a powerful, meaningful impact for others through your work.

Mars in the 11th House of Friendship and Community Outreach:
Working with groups of people to help them move forward into the future in a better way using your unique skills.

Mars in the 12th House of Spirituality and Higher Purpose:
Committing yourself to a higher vision or mission that feels deeply important to you on a soul level.

4
Jupiter: Your Greatest Joy

Work does not have to be a word that only means "hard labor." Work can be light, fun, interesting, and even invigorating when you are channeling your energy into the type of projects that make your eyes light up and your heart flutter. As the planet of opportunity, expansion, and abundance, Jupiter can explain what brings you the most excitement so that you can center your work around that.

Jupiter is often the fan-favorite planet because it signifies our greatest joy in life and the things we can't wait to work on. Not only do we have more energy when do what we love, but our expansive, optimistic energy can also spread to others and inspire them to grow. Find your Jupiter Sign and House to discover what you can do to bring the most joy and abundance to yourself and others through your work.

Jupiter Retrograde: Every year, lasting for about four months, Jupiter appears to move backwards in the sky as it goes through its annual retrograde period. Those born during Jupiter Retrograde may have trouble deciding which of their projects will garner the most joy and excitement. They will need to dive in and play with their ideas to determine what will bring them the most happiness because they often cannot logically analyze it from the outside looking in.

Soul Lesson: Too much of a good thing is not always a good thing. Take time to sort through your options so you can focus on the opportunities that feel most exhilarating.

JUPITER IN ARIES

Work feels the most fun for those with Jupiter in Aries when they are coming up with fresh ideas and motivating others by taking the lead. They feel the most excited when they're first starting a new project or promoting a new discovery that has recently captured their attention. Their love of beating the competition drives them to do bigger and better things with each project they embark on. It's often best for them to choose work where things move at a fast pace and each day holds something different and new.

JUPITER IN TAURUS

The greatest excitement for Jupiter in Taurus comes from pouring quality care into their work. They love to calmly take their time to create something sustainable that will support them and others for a long time to come. They are often most delighted by working with their five senses: taking in beautiful sights, sounds, tastes, textures, and smells and sharing them through their work. Their sense of joy also stems from creating solid avenues for revenue to flow to them so they can continue to be a strong, supportive force in others' lives.

JUPITER IN GEMINI

Jupiter in Gemini people love to share their ideas and work in collaborative environments where they can become part of a greater conversation. Their greatest joy comes from passing along information, tips, and resources that make life easier or better for others, even if they're simply sharing a collection of things they've researched or overheard. They have many different and varied interests, so having multiple creative outlets to express sides of themselves is key for them to feel happy in their work.

JUPITER IN CANCER

Jupiter in Cancer gets the most excited when they can nurture and care for other people. With a strong craving for close emotional connections, their heart buzzes when they can help another person feel safe and protected by providing a space for them to air their feelings and find the best solution. When they do, they also get more opportunities to receive joy from others in return. Being around familiar people, in comfortable spaces, and reflecting on the past to create a better future are a few of the things that can make their work feel more like fun.

JUPITER IN LEO

Jupiter in Leo gets lit up by presenting their talents and seeking to become the best at whatever they most love to do. They get the most excited when they are putting in the work to come out on top by pouring their heart into one big passion project. Incredibly generous in sharing their energy and resources, Jupiter in Leo naturally inspires and commands others' attention when they use their larger-than-life presence to bring out the best in others. Children, games, sports or fitness, and anything fun, light-hearted, colorful, dramatic, or creative brings them joy.

JUPITER IN VIRGO

The quest for purity and perfection is what brings Jupiter in Virgo the most excitement. When they are using their work to help others find the best solution to a complex problem, remove blocks, create better habits, or cleanse impurities, they joyfully thrive. Cultivating supportive rituals for themselves in their own lives can be just as rewarding, but it is possible to go overboard in making things too precise. This sign feels the greatest joy when they savor the everyday maintenance tasks that keep them feeling balanced, empowered, and energetically equipped to continue providing excellent service to others.

JUPITER IN LIBRA

Jupiter in Libra gets the most excited when they can bring a sense of harmony, beauty, or peace to others' lives. Their charming nature wins them many friends because they are often willing to go above and beyond to please others. It brings them the greatest joy to make another person smile or to bring justice to an unfair situation. They also love to use their sense of artistry to dress up and make their environment look nice or to bring out the beauty in another.

JUPITER IN SCORPIO

Jupiter in Scorpio loves getting to the bottom of things to better understand another person or to solve a problem. They get the most excited when they can create a change or transformation by solving a mystery or when they ingrain themselves in a quest to unveil the truth about something that is normally taboo or hidden. Although their intensity can be a lot for others to handle, they experience the greatest joy when they pour themselves fully into their deeper passions. Sometimes that means burning down others' expectations in the process.

JUPITER IN SAGITTARIUS

Work feels the most fun to Jupiter in Sagittarius when it takes them on a learning adventure. Their greatest joy is in getting out of their normal bubble of everyday life to discover what else is out there in the form of travel to faraway places, reading books, taking courses, and going down the rabbit hole of their own quest for self-discovery. What is even more exciting to them than pursuing their many interests, however, is being able to open others' eyes to new ideas and experiences by reaching back to share their philosophy based on what they have learned.

JUPITER IN CAPRICORN

For Jupiter in Capricorn, getting on track with their master plan is what makes life feel most fun. Hard work can be like a form of therapy for them, and often there is nothing more satisfying to them than checking off one of their many to-do's. This sign's greatest joy is in making progress toward a worthy goal and having their hard work recognized so they can be seen as an authority in their field. These powerhouses can achieve anything they set their mind to as long as they're doing it for an important purpose that brings them excitement.

JUPITER IN AQUARIUS

Those born with Jupiter in Aquarius love to challenge convention by putting a unique spin on their work. They feel the most excited when they can create revolutionary change by spreading new-age, cutting-edge ideas that many in the mainstream have never heard of or seen. At the same time, they are humanitarians and natural-born activists who are brave enough to revolt against inequality. When they can use their work to bring important information to others in their community surrounding a common cause, they are harnessing their greatest joy.

JUPITER IN PISCES

The greatest excitement for Jupiter in Pisces comes from envisioning creative ideas that will allow them to inspire and maybe even heal others. They feel the most joy when they can bring more magic or meaning to others' lives as part of their own greater soul mission. This sign's imaginative essence naturally influences others to dream bigger. Their ability to see the potential in another person is unparalleled. Although their sensitivity to others' emotions can be used as a healing superpower, the outside world can sometimes feel like too much, leading them to need extra time alone to recharge.

Jupiter in the Houses

You feel the most excited when you are...

Jupiter in the 1st House of
Identity, Authenticity, and Leadership:
Getting acknowledged for being your true self and standing up as a powerful leader or role model who influences others.

Jupiter in the 2nd House of Values, Desires, and Goal Setting:
Manifesting your desires in life and encouraging other people to go after their goals, too.

Jupiter in the 3rd House of Social Networking:
Sharing your ideas and interests freely with others and having compelling conversations through your work.

Jupiter in the 4th House of Home, Family, and Long-term Security:
Cultivating a rich home and family life or holding space for others to help them feel safe and comforted.

Jupiter in the 5th House of Fun and Creativity:
Coming up with fun, original ideas to bring more light-hearted joy to others' lives through expressing your child-like creative essence.

Jupiter in the 6th House of Health, Work, and Daily Rituals:
Making everyday life easier, more enjoyable, or efficient by removing whatever is getting in the way of feeling more whole or in control.

Jupiter in the 7th House of
Relationships and One-on-one Work:
Supporting others by working closely with them to find
solutions to their problems and needs.

Jupiter in the 8th House of
Business, Finance, and Shadow Work:
Taking ownership over how you spend your time and earn your
money and diving deep to understand blocks and insecurities.

Jupiter in the 9th House of
Education, Exploration, and Self-discovery:
Diving into a new subject or area of focus that sparks your curiosity
and sharing what you learn with others as you go.

Jupiter in the 10th House of Career and Higher Calling:
Using your top skills and talents to spread positive ripple effects to
others through your career.

Jupiter in the 11th House of
Friendship and Community Outreach:
Supporting your community by bringing people together around a
common cause to improve life for each other in the future.

Jupiter in the 12th House of Spirituality and Higher Purpose:
Being aligned with a greater vision of how you wish the world would
be and making attaining that your life's work.

Saturn: Your Greatest Challenge

The planet Saturn brings to our lives the major constrictions and tough challenges that force us to mature and grow. This strict teacher planet symbolizes our greater need to take our soul mission seriously and to be focused and disciplined about carrying it out. Your Saturn soul mission is thought to be based on your past life karma as well as on certain lessons you promised yourself you would finally learn in this lifetime. Although it may seem like a negative force because of the immense sense of pressure it brings, working in tune with your Saturn Sign and House will ultimately bring you the biggest rewards and benefits in the long run.

Saturn Retrograde: Those born during Saturn Retrograde, which occurs annually and lasts about four and a half months, are often confused about their long-term goals. They are the most likely to need help finding their purpose. It is often hidden from them until they do the work to uncover it themselves. The master plan of their life will most likely never magically reveal itself, so they need to create clarity by trying things out and experimenting with their ideas.

Soul Lesson: Take more time to test out your ideas to find your focus. Clarity can only be created by looking back, not forward.

SATURN IN ARIES

Saturn in Aries is meant to challenge themselves to assert their own individual perspective. They are learning to stand up for themselves and to come up with a fresh way of doing things that is not inspired by other people but instead by their own inventiveness and passion for doing what they love. Because Aries is not a sign that typically sticks with projects for very long after the sense of newness wears off, they need to learn to have discipline in propelling their unique point of view forward instead of letting other distractions get in the way.

SATURN IN TAURUS

Saturn in Taurus has a strong need to build a foundation that is steady and sustainable to provide for themselves and others far into the future. They are being called to have more patience and persistence when putting effort into projects that may not come to culmination for a long time. It is also important for these people to create a life and work situation that nourishes them while they are working toward their goals by gearing what they do around something that makes them feel good along their journey to success.

SATURN IN GEMINI

Those who were born with Saturn in Gemini are here to learn how to share their ideas and collaborate with others more cohesively. Their biggest challenge is getting into the minds of other people so they can present their message in a way that will resonate the most. This may involve getting out of their comfort zone to connect with new people or even creating a network of their own to bring people together around a common topic. It is also key for them to surround themselves with the right people who can best help them reach their goals.

SATURN IN CANCER

The biggest challenge for Saturn in Cancer revolves around creating a firm foundation for their future comfort and emotional security. This might include being disciplined in forging stronger connections with family, creating a satisfying home life, or earning consistent income that can support the personal goals and milestones they are working toward. A big part of their challenge also involves being more caring, kind, and compassionate toward others as well as making the people they care about feel safe, seen, and protected, too.

SATURN IN LEO

Saturn in Leo people have the life challenge of becoming bolder and more confident in presenting their original creative ideas. They are here to learn how to become the best at their chosen craft so they can eventually stand out as a positive role model or trusted expert others can look up to. They need to work hard to gain recognition and appreciation by creating the things they wish existed in the world. To do so, they need to stop undervaluing themselves and underestimating what they are capable of producing.

SATURN IN VIRGO

People with Saturn in Virgo are here to learn how to cultivate consistent habits and routines that help their lives and work flow more smoothly. There may be a lot of chaos in their lives before they learn how to support themselves with better organization and a schedule. Taking care of the tasks that will make them feel focused and organized lets them do better work. This sign is also learning how to become more detail-oriented in refining and polishing their projects without letting their drive for perfectionism stop them from moving forward at all.

SATURN IN LIBRA

The biggest challenge for Saturn in Libra is all about bringing greater harmony into their dealings with others as well as into their overall experience of life. This may mean they need to work especially hard to cultivate relationships that are built on reciprocity, where neither side is feeling like they are giving or taking too much. It also involves spending a great deal of time and energy creating the ideal balance between life and work, creating balance between the mind and the body, and even making sure the energy of their own home and work environment is pleasing.

SATURN IN SCORPIO

Saturn in Scorpio must become dedicated to unveiling the deeper reasons why they hold themselves back from greater success. Their biggest challenge is to cultivate a sense of discipline around pursuing their deeper passions instead of simply settling for work that keeps their focus on surface-level subject matters that don't drive or motivate them. They will need to constantly learn to shed what is not in alignment with how they want to feel and reinvent themselves to bring more of their true nature into the way they show up for work.

SATURN IN SAGITTARIUS

The biggest challenge for Saturn in Sagittarius is to find their own answers instead of relying on other teachers, experts, or gurus to give them guidance on how to live. They are here to discover their own belief system that is free from the thoughts or opinions of others. At the same time, they may never feel like they know enough to become an expert themselves and will seek out additional degrees or certifications to prove their wisdom is sound. They need to learn that their valuable life experiences alone can qualify them to teach and guide others.

SATURN IN CAPRICORN

Saturn in Capricorn needs to become more disciplined around goal setting by creating a system, program, or path that they—and eventually others—can follow to achieve their aims as efficiently as possible. They may feel a strong pressure to achieve greater levels of status, success, and security and to prove themselves as an authority figure in their industry. It is easy for them to feel like their hard work is never enough, and they can overwhelm themselves easily until they learn to pace themselves and break down their goals.

SATURN IN AQUARIUS

The ultimate challenge for Saturn in Aquarius is to become more forward-thinking and innovative. Instead of taking everything they are told at face value, they must go out in search of their own answers. This is how they can find the best possible solutions to issues that are facing their community or the greater world. The hardest part of this lesson is that they must be willing to stand up for the causes that are most important to them, even if it means being misunderstood or rejected, because not everyone may be ready to hear the alternative perspectives they propose.

SATURN IN PISCES

Those born with Saturn in Pisces must learn to use their intuition as a guide in everything they do. Their greatest challenge is in harnessing their sensitive nature like an inner GPS to make sure they are living and working in alignment with a greater mission that feels meaningful to their soul. It is important for them to work hard to make their vision come true instead of simply imagining it or daydreaming about it. This goal may involve helping others get into greater energetic alignment with their emotional or spiritual nature, too.

Saturn in the Houses

Your biggest life challenge revolves around...

**Saturn in the 1st House of
Identity, Authenticity, and Leadership:**
Asserting yourself as an independent individual or leader who lives
and works on their own terms.

Saturn in the 2nd House of Values, Desires, and Goal Setting:
Aligning your life and work with your true values, increasing your
self-worth, and focusing on your personal goals.

Saturn in the 3rd House of Social Networking:
Expressing your thoughts and ideas more freely and collaborating
with others to reach your goals faster.

**Saturn in the 4th House of
Home, Family, and Long-term Security:**
Creating a stable and rich personal life so that you can feel
comfortable far into the future.

Saturn in the 5th House of Fun and Creativity:
Working hard to create the things you wish existed in the world and
learning how to be playful and have more fun.

Saturn in the 6th House of Health, Work, and Daily Rituals:
Setting up consistent routines that support you in doing your best
work and keeping your overall wellbeing balanced.

Saturn in the 7th House of Relationships and One-on-one Work:
Cultivating harmonious relationships with others and prioritizing helping others with their needs.

Saturn in the 8th House of
Business, Finance, and Shadow Work:
Being strategic in pursuing your deeper desires by unveiling what holds you back in your subconscious mind.

Saturn in the 9th House of
Education, Exploration, and Self-discovery:
Endlessly learning about the things that interest you the most and sharing them with others.

Saturn in the 10th House of Career and Higher Calling:
Elevating your status, authority, and professional reputation while creating a powerful, widespread impact on others.

Saturn in the 11th House of
Friendship and Community Outreach:
Bringing people together around a common cause to make the world a better place for your community in your own special way.

Saturn in the 12th House of Spirituality and Higher Purpose:
Releasing limiting beliefs or fears that have been weighing on you and holding you back from doing what you really want to do.

Uranus: What Makes You Unique

Uranus is the planet of rebellion, challenging the status quo, going against the grain, and doing things in your own special way. We all have something about ourselves that makes us seem a little bit different or maybe even quirky compared to the people who surround us. Instead of trying to dull yourself down to fit in, Uranus helps us learn to use our quirks to our advantage—to stand out and spark a wave of change and innovation. Your Uranus Sign and House is where you break convention because you prefer to dance to the beat of your own drum instead of syncing to whatever is currently popular or mainstream.

Uranus Retrograde: Lasting for about five months of every year, it is relatively more common to be born with Uranus Retrograde than with the retrograde of most of the other planets before it. It may be difficult for these people to do things differently from other people around them, or they may have trouble understanding what makes them unique. They may be confused when they need to make a big change and may need to take extra time to think things through when doing something different or new.

Soul Lesson: You are learning how to more mindfully regulate your energy by going on a discovery process to figure out how to most effectively create change without being too much of a follower or a rebel.

URANUS IN ARIES

Uranus in Aries is rebellious to the core. If someone tells them they cannot do something, you can be sure they will find a way. What makes them unique is their inventiveness for new ideas and their strong willingness to take risks that others wouldn't dare. Their impulsive nature can lead to the greatest invention or the worst trouble. Preferring to blaze their own trail both in life and in work, they will need to learn from their own mistakes. They detest it when others try to step in or get in their way.

URANUS IN TAURUS

Those born with Uranus in Taurus can be especially stubborn. They take their sweet time to move forward and cannot be rushed. Once they have decided on their strategy, however, they are impossible to stop. This sign is incredibly resourceful. They have a strong desire to build a steady, sustainable future. The way they do this, and the way they choose to earn their money, is often radically different from others. They are here to reinvent traditional values and create practical, lasting change in the world, but they do so on their own terms.

URANUS IN GEMINI

Uranus in Gemini is restless and quick-moving. They are incredibly fast learners and make great thought leaders with their gift for communicating their own unique spin. With multiple interests and a love for staying busy, they are unlikely to master any one subject because they change their minds so often. They have many unusual friends and connections that bridge across their plentiful interests. This sign is here to collect data so they can plant a new seed for social change. However, their ideas are so unique, they may be unacceptable to the general population at first.

URANUS IN CANCER

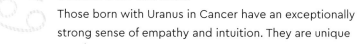

Those born with Uranus in Cancer have an exceptionally strong sense of empathy and intuition. They are unique because they care so much about fighting for others' needs, especially the needs of those who are undervalued or ignored by society. At the same time, they may not get along with their own family or anyone who tries to force them into old traditions that dictate how they should live their life. This sign has their own unique perspective on how to run their home and seek to challenge how a normal family should look.

URANUS IN LEO

Uranus in Leo has a desire to rebel that comes through in their willingness to stand in the spotlight as a leader or role model for their creative ideas. Bold and confident in sharing their unique self-expression, this sign is not afraid to be someone who stands out from the crowd in their work. Although others may sometimes see them as over-dramatic attention seekers, their strong personality allows them to show others the magic that can happen when you take a strong stand for your own beliefs, opinions, and talents.

URANUS IN VIRGO

Uranus in Virgo has an exceptional talent for noticing the details and understanding the inner workings of an issue or project they are drawn to working on. Although others may find them to be overly picky, this unique talent for noticing what is not working and how things could be done better can be used as an incredible superpower in the right setting. They make great researchers, analysts, scientists, and healers, as they are inspired by the natural world to bring about greater purity and higher efficiency standards through their work.

URANUS IN LIBRA

Uranus in Libra's uniqueness comes from their ability to bring harmony to chaotic situations with a sense of artistry and flair. They have no patience for situations in which people are being treated unjustly and will go to great lengths to fight for solutions that they feel are the fairest. At the same time, their unconventional perspective on partnership can sometimes bring them trouble in both business and personal relationships. Although they are generally tolerant of others with different beliefs, they feel the need to protect their own independence to stay in their creative flow.

URANUS IN SCORPIO

Those born with Uranus in Scorpio have deep and probing minds. Incredibly determined, they will stop at nothing to achieve their aims when they are passionate about a project. They are here to bring a shock to societal systems by uncovering the truth about what goes on in the shadows. Because of this, they make excellent researchers, detectives, and documentarians. Sometimes known to cut corners to get where they want to be faster, their uniqueness comes from their ability to strategize the swiftest solution to widespread problems through their work.

URANUS IN SAGITTARIUS

Uranus in Sagittarius is on an endless quest for knowledge and new experiences. However, this sign is not interested in following any established teachers or gurus and instead seeks out their own answers in everything they do. Their unique power comes from their willingness to dive deep to uncover the truth of why we are here and what we are meant to do. Independent thinkers, they can be quite blunt because authenticity is more important to them than making friends. They will fiercely protect their sense of freedom at all costs.

URANUS IN CAPRICORN

Uranus in Capricorn is incredibly ambitious and hard-working. They will go to great lengths to devise better systems and structures than what has conventionally been passed down. Their uniqueness comes not only from the practical and efficient solutions they devise but also from the extent to which they will work to make their dreams real. They have a superpower in planning ahead to anticipate future problems. However, they can also be quite critical when it comes to measuring the quality of work—both their own work and that of others.

URANUS IN AQUARIUS

For Uranus in Aquarius, rebelling comes very naturally. They are forward-thinking individuals who prefer to go against the grain simply because it's fun. Even if it is quite shocking to the people around them, they are happiest when doing things differently from what has already been done. They have eccentric minds that see things from a perspective that may be far before their time. What makes this sign most unique, however, is their willingness to shift and change the world for the betterment of society and the radical improvement of others' lives.

URANUS IN PISCES

Uranus in Pisces has an otherworldly and imaginative nature that is unparalleled. They are often more in touch with other, subconscious realms than they are with the current state of their reality. What makes them especially different is their ability to see the bigger picture and their willingness to create and live in their own dream world. This sign has the power to create immense shifts in the spiritual belief patterns of others as they learn to have faith in themselves and the supportive nature of the universe.

Uranus in the Houses

You rebel the most when it comes to...

Uranus in the 1st House of
Identity, Authenticity, and Leadership:
How you lead and influence others simply by showing up
as your most authentic self.

Uranus in the 2nd House of Values, Desires, and Goal Setting:
Going after your goals, manifesting your desires, and attracting what
you need and want out of life.

Uranus in the 3rd House of Social Networking:
How you communicate with others, the company you choose to
keep, and the way you share your ideas to influence social change.

Uranus in the 4th House of
Home, Family, and Long-term Security:
Creating a unique personal lifestyle that goes against what is
considered normal in the mainstream.

Uranus in the 5th House of Fun and Creativity:
How you have fun and express your original ideas with the goal of
creating new inventions that have never been seen.

Uranus in the 6th House of Health, Work, and Daily Rituals:
How you live and work day-to-day and the way you take
care of your health and overall wellbeing.

Uranus in the 7th House of
Relationships and One-on-one Work:

The people you are drawn to being in relationship with
or the way you choose to support others.

Uranus in the 8th House of
Business, Finance, and Shadow Work:

How you earn your money and your willingness to unroot and
understand your deeper insecurities.

Uranus in the 9th House of
Education, Exploration, and Self-discovery:

Seeking out the answers of the universe to determine your own
belief system and sharing it with others.

Uranus in the 10th House of Career and Higher Calling:

How you portray yourself to the public or the work you do to make a
powerful impact through your career.

Uranus in the 11th House of
Friendship and Community Outreach:

Standing up for the concerns of others and rallying a unique group of
people around a common cause.

Uranus in the 12th House of Spirituality and Higher Purpose:

Tapping into your imagination or intuition to become more
connected to a bigger soul mission.

Neptune: Your Dream Vision

When you look into the future, what do you most hope to see? What would you like your life to be? The planet Neptune rules over our dreams and ideals as well as illusions and delusions. On the chart, it lays out your beliefs on how you wish the world could be if it was possible to experience heaven on earth. When it comes to creating the bigger impact you want to make, it's important to first make sure you are clear on your vision of how you want the future to look. Otherwise, how will you know where you are going if you can't imagine the ideal outcome you want to bring about? By reading your Neptune Sign and House, you can clarify the life you are hoping to create—not only for yourself but also for others—through your life's work.

Neptune Retrograde: Those born during Neptune Retrograde, which occurs annually for about five months each time, may feel especially unclear on their dream vision for the future, but astrology can help narrow it down. They may either have no idea what they want for their future or they have many different dreams that rarely stay the same long enough to be completely followed through.

Soul Lesson: You may never have a totally clear idea of which direction you want to head or which dream is most worth pursuing. Take action anyway. Clarity comes from reflecting back on what has felt closest to your idea of heaven and releasing what does not.

NEPTUNE IN ARIES

Those born with Neptune in Aries strongly believe in the power and importance of us all being unique individuals. They want to help create a world in which everyone can pursue their true passions and be appreciated for their unique perspective. These people are bold visionaries and are not afraid to stand up for their beliefs, even if it means they have to be forceful or even aggressive. They move quickly when going after their desires and believe no one should take no for an answer when faced with obstacles that could take them away from doing what they really love.

NEPTUNE IN TAURUS

The dream that Neptune in Taurus has for the future centers around creating a more beautiful and sustainable world that is also more pleasing to the five senses. Although they can be materialistic and obsessed with collecting possessions, their dreams are usually quite practical in nature because they are also very resourceful. They desire to create a supportive, stable environment for themselves and others, although they may sometimes become disillusioned by ignoring others' needs to do things their own way.

NEPTUNE IN GEMINI

Neptune in Gemini dreams of a world in which others can be connected to the information they need and can freely share their thoughts and ideas among a greater network. As conceptual thinkers themselves, they also love to champion others' unique ideas. This sign makes inspiring teachers and writers, even if the points they try to make are not always the most practical. They may have many different dreams that conflict with one another, which can sometimes confuse people as they quickly change their stance.

NEPTUNE IN CANCER

Neptune in Cancer cares deeply about the plight of others. They desire to live in a world in which everyone is well taken care of and no one gets left behind. With a love for championing human rights, their emotions can over-take them when they see that someone else is suffering. It is important for them not only to make someone else feel better but to create a long-term plan that will allow them to continually support themselves enough to be able to sustainably give back.

NEPTUNE IN LEO

Those born with Neptune in Leo love to champion creativity. Play and fun is important to them, and they seek to enrich others' lives by helping them bring out their own inner children. As natural-born leaders, they want to create a world in which others can feel more fearless, bold, and confident when expressing their talents. They may do well in the arts and entertainment industry, where their over-the-top ideas can have a chance to become realized for the enjoyment of others. Whatever creative outlet they choose to pursue, they dream of coming out on top as the best.

NEPTUNE IN VIRGO

Neptune in Virgo is enamored with purifying the body, working intelligently, and honoring the natural world through healthy eating and cutting down on wastefulness. They dream of a world in which everyone has their basic needs met with nothing more or less than what is required to live a well-balanced and healthy life. Feeling their best is important to them because they want to show up and be of the highest service to others. Although they can be staunch perfectionists, they also notice and appreciate the wonderful nuances in even the smallest things.

NEPTUNE IN LIBRA

Neptune in Libra's sense of idealism centers around creating a fairer world. They will go far out of their way to support another person facing unjust circumstances even it means inconveniencing themselves. This is a sign that wants to live in a world that is beautiful, harmonious, and tolerant to opposing views. They long to live and work in pleasing environments that allow them to be a supportive voice for others. At the same time, they can have trouble making their own decisions without another person to bounce their ideas off.

NEPTUNE IN SCORPIO

Neptune in Scorpio is unafraid of peering into the darker side of life. They desire to create a world in which deeper secrets are revealed because they can be quite obsessive in their pursuit to uncover hidden truths. Intrigued by unsolved mysteries, the mystical, and depth psychology, they seek to get to the core of what holds others back from creating necessary transformation and change. Whatever their current dream may be, they will be intensely driven in their pursuit to make it real. At the same time, they can be secretive and may dislike sharing their true motive with others.

NEPTUNE IN SAGITTARIUS

Those born with Neptune in Sagittarius dream of exploring new ideas and embracing foreign cultures. With a grand sense of optimism, they seek to live in a world in which there are endless opportunities to discover new information and have interesting and unique experiences. They may also enjoy opening others up to new worlds by sharing the places, ideas, and pieces of knowledge that have inspired them most. Honoring their own authentic truth is one of their top ideals, and they seek to help others learn to do the same.

NEPTUNE IN CAPRICORN

People with Neptune in Capricorn are in pursuit of the perfect plan. They dream of a world that is free of chaos, and they seek to create it by using their strong work ethic to come up with the most practical and proactive plans to create controlled outcomes. Although they easily inspire others with their ability to come up with complex systems to make things more efficient, their high standards for their work can also make them prone to crippling perfectionism if they are not careful to take a step back and remind themselves of what is really most important.

NEPTUNE IN AQUARIUS

Neptune in Aquarius envisions a world in which everyone is focused on creating a more innovative and equal future. They seek to improve civilization through embracing new technology, new-age spirituality, humanitarianism, and innovative science. They also want each person's unique differences to be celebrated rather than being grounds for rejection. This sign has a special talent for bringing people together around a common cause even though their own personal ideals may be unconventional or eccentric.

NEPTUNE IN PISCES

Those with Neptune in Pisces constantly seek the higher meaning behind their purpose for being alive. Because they have one of the strongest imaginations of any of the signs and their ability to empathize with others is unparalleled, they are here to create a world in which communing with our spiritual and intuitive nature to dismantle suffering becomes the norm. Their greatest dream is for others to learn to harness their emotions as a guide for their actions instead of ignoring how they feel to uncomfortably press on with business as usual while perpetuating a way of life that is uninspiring and out of alignment.

Neptune in the Houses

Your dream vision for the future revolves around...

Neptune in the 1st House of
Identity, Authenticity, and Leadership:
Becoming a unique leader as you embody the change
you want to see in the world.

Neptune in the 2nd House of Values, Desires, and Goal Setting:
Being able to manifest all your desires for love, money, or beauty
without settling for less than what is truly ideal.

Neptune in the 3rd House of Social Networking:
Connecting people to share ideas, resources, and solutions that can
make the world a better place for all.

Neptune in the 4th House of
Home, Family,and Long-term Security:
Cultivating a rich personal life and a comfortable environment
surrounded by loved ones.

Neptune in the 5th House of Fun and Creativity:
Coming up with creative and original ideas that inspire
and ignite others' creativity, too.

Neptune in the 6th House of Health, Work, and Daily Rituals:
Attaining perfection through healthy habits and supportive routines
that make everyday life easier, more efficient, or more enjoyable.

**Neptune in the 7th House of
Relationships and One-on-one Work:**
Creating more loving, equal, and balanced partnerships between
yourself and others as well as helping others do the same.

**Neptune in the 8th House of
Business, Finance, and Shadow Work:**
Earning your money by pursuing your deepest
desires on your own terms.

**Neptune in the 9th House of
Education, Exploration, and Self-discovery:**
Engaging in endless learning and sharing your
discoveries to expand others' minds.

Neptune in the 10th House of Career and Higher Calling:
Attaining the heights of career success so you can make a
widespread impact on others.

**Neptune in the 11th House of
Friendship and Community Outreach:**
Bringing people together to improve the community while
supporting important causes that affect others.

Neptune in the 12th House of Spirituality and Higher Purpose:
Creating a society in which people are more connected to their
inner knowing and higher soul mission.

Pluto: Your Soul's Evolution

Pluto is the planet of transformation, evolution, death, and rebirth. True to its energetic signature, it was essentially "killed off" itself when it was downgraded from a planet to instead being labeled a dwarf planet by the International Astronomical Union in 2006. Even though astronomers technically no longer classify it as a planet, astrologers still know Pluto to be one of the strongest, most intense, and most powerful forces we can track on a chart.

Pluto symbolizes our need to overcome our greatest fears, which, when faced, unlock a new level of evolution for us. Even more importantly, however, this point on your chart describes how you can make the biggest difference for others through your life's work in a way that powerfully evolves and transforms the world around you. We each have the capability to inspire widespread change in our own way. Your Pluto Sign and House will illuminate the area of your life in that brings the greatest breakdown and breakthrough as you bust through your fears and learn how to better channel your personal power to benefit the world.

Pluto Retrograde: Lasting nearly five and a half months of the year, Pluto is the most common planet to fall in retrograde on a chart. Those born when the planet of rebirth was in retrograde go through a deep transformational process within themselves and their own mind or psyche over the course of their lives. This deep psychological shift is what causes them to be able to help create change for others. These people may be unclear about who they're growing into, how to best harness their power, or what the next level of their evolving life or work will look like ahead of time. It is more of a natural process of tuning in and letting the old fall away as they face their fears along the way.

Soul Lesson: Trust your intuition and be willing to let go of what's not working in your work when it's time to let go, even if it is uncomfortable or doesn't make sense to others.

PLUTO IN ARIES

Pluto in Aries grows the most when they are putting themselves first. They are here to learn how to stand up for themselves and their bright ideas even in the face of difficulty or other people's opposition. Pluto in Aries makes the biggest difference in transforming others' lives when they are motivating others to act on their ideas and to harness their passions to become the lit-up leaders of their own lives. They have the power to ignite others to step forward and own their individuality.

PLUTO IN TAURUS

Those born with Pluto in Taurus best harness their power when they are taking control of establishing their own sense of stability to create a life of beauty and abundance for themselves. The quest to support themselves and give themselves what they need in life may bring up many deep-seated fears around survival. However, the more they push through their blocks to find a practical way to earn money and get what they need to feel safe, the more they can powerfully inspire others to believe that they can do the same.

PLUTO IN GEMINI

The biggest fear for Pluto in Gemini to overcome centers around sharing their ideas more freely with the people surrounding them. In the beginning, they may worry that others will not think they know what they are talking about and doubt their expertise. Once this sign learns to speak up for themselves and confidently communicate their needs and thoughts without censoring them, they will be able to transform others' lives by influencing them to do the same.

PLUTO IN CANCER

Pluto in Cancer can have a strong fear to overcome around how to handle themselves when not knowing what the future will bring. They tend to worry greatly about the prospect of change until they realize that they have the power and strength to become their own caregiver and to turn their future into anything they want it to become. By learning how to honor their own needs for comfort and stability, they can help others learn to release heavy emotions and own their ability to protect and nourish themselves.

PLUTO IN LEO

Pluto in Leo changes the world by being a way-shower. They are here to learn how to harness their natural leadership skills and confidently share their talents for the benefit of bringing out the best in others. At first, they may fear judgment for or rejection from showing up to express their creativity. However, as they work through this obstacle for themselves, they inspire massive change in others' lives by lighting the way forward for those who have a similar fear.

PLUTO IN VIRGO

The evolutionary need of Pluto in Virgo is to bring order to areas of life that feel chaotic. All the details can be overwhelming, with the attainment of perfection feeling nearly impossible at first. However, as they work step by step to remove the blocks or even emotional barriers that get in the way of creating an easier, heathier, or more efficient life, they gain the power to influence others and show them how to do the same.

PLUTO IN LIBRA

Pluto in Libra is here to become a seeker of justice.

Easily seeing the opposing perspectives of both sides of an issue, they may get lost in fearful indecision, which keeps them from contributing to creating a fairer and more balanced world. As they learn to step back and stop focusing their attention on solving problems that feel exhausting or depressing, they naturally show others how to embrace the beauty, peace, and harmony already surrounding them.

PLUTO IN SCORPIO

The greatest evolution for Pluto in Scorpio comes from being willing to dive deep to uncover the root cause of fear itself. As they go through dark and emotional times in their early life, they eventually come to realize it is only themselves that holds them back. Once they learn to face their fears and become more adaptable in transforming any heaviness or discomfort, they can change the world by sharing the tools they have used to help others bring light to their own inner shadows.

PLUTO IN SAGITTARIUS

Pluto in Sagittarius's drive for transformation stems from a need to understand how to operate in full alignment with their inner truth. Unable to express themselves authentically at first, they learn how painful it is to hide from who they really are. The more they allow themselves to be completely honest about who they are, the more they can live in greater alignment with their true beliefs. That helps them inspire others to create transformational change in their own lives.

PLUTO IN CAPRICORN

Those born with Pluto in Capricorn are here to learn about self-control. They are here to face their fears by crafting a methodical strategy to move out of chaos and on to a well-ordered path that takes them in the direction of their long-term goals. As they find the organizational structures that work for them, they transform the world by allowing others to benefit from following the path they pave along their way.

PLUTO IN AQUARIUS

Those born with Pluto in Aquarius are here to challenge the systems and structures that were built before their time. Although they may begin life feeling afraid to show off their differences in case they will no longer be accepted, they eventually learn that no one changes the world by fitting in. Their greatest ability to inspire transformation is by showing others how incredibly powerful it is to confidently stand out and spark a new perspective.

PLUTO IN PISCES

The greatest fear for Pluto in Pisces comes from surrendering to the powerful forces of the universe. Often, they are born into the world with a lack of faith in something greater, and they will need to do a lot of soul searching to understand their purpose in life. By using their emotions as a guide on how to move closer toward their soul's calling, they not only find their higher mission but also inspire many others to believe in the power of their intuition.

Pluto in the Houses

Reminder: By learning to grow in these ways, you can transform others' lives by showing them how to do the same. Your greatest need for growth and evolution centers around...

Pluto in the 1st House of
Identity, Authenticity, and Leadership:
Asserting yourself as an individual and constantly shedding old versions of yourself that no longer serve you.

Pluto in the 2nd House of Values, Desires, and Goal Setting:
Learning to believe in your worthiness and your capacity to receive the things you want and need in life.

Pluto in the 3rd House of Social Networking:
Speaking up to share your ideas and trusting that you know enough to have something valuable to share with others.

Pluto in the 4th House of
Home, Family, and Long-term Security:
Creating your own foundation for stability and comfort by becoming your own caregiver.

Pluto in the 5th House of Fun and Creativity:
Creating the things you wish existed in your life and work instead of waiting for others to make life better.

Pluto in the 6th House of Health, Work, and Daily Rituals:
Taking care of yourself and your daily needs so you can support yourself in feeling your best.

Pluto in the 7th House of Relationships and One-on-one Work:
Creating an equal balance in relationships instead of allowing one person to overpower or receive less than the other.

Pluto in the 8th House of Business, Finance, and Shadow Work:
Diving deep to understand where your fears are holding you back from creating greater financial and emotional security.

**Pluto in the 9th House of
Education, Exploration, and Self-discovery:**
Looking beyond the world you see around you to explore what else is out there and expand your personal belief system.

Pluto in the 10th House of Career and Higher Calling:
Allowing yourself to be seen by the public sharing your gifts and talents to make a powerful impact on others.

Pluto in the 11th House of Friendship and Community Outreach:
Finding or creating a sense of belonging in your community and overcoming a fear of rejection.

Pluto in the 12th House of Spirituality and Higher Purpose:
Developing a deeper connection with your emotional and intuitive nature and releasing limiting beliefs.

CHAPTER 4

Uncovering Your Deeper Soul-Level Motivations

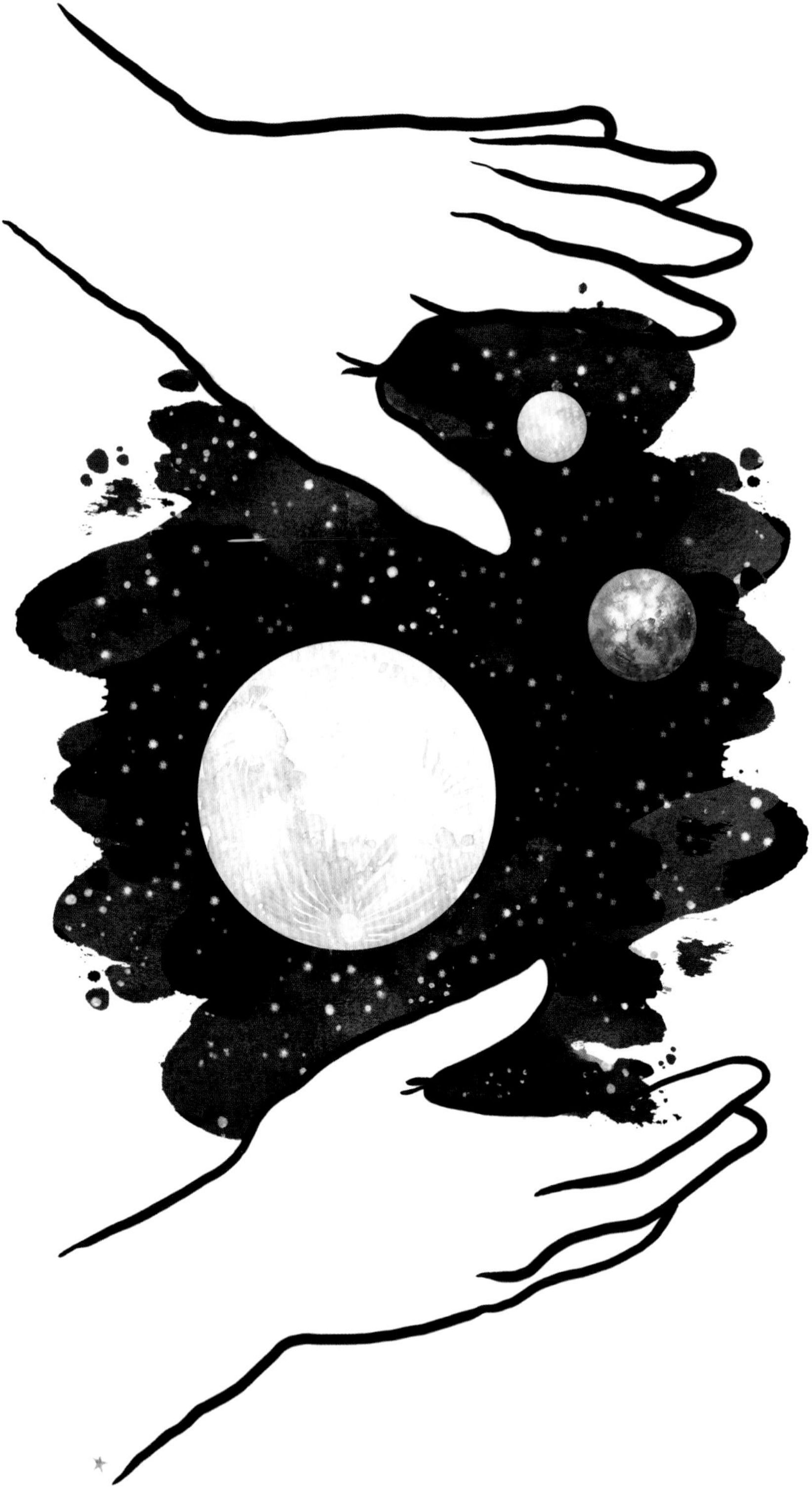

While the planets describe your outward behavior, there are also tens of thousands of other non-planetary points that can be tracked on an astrological chart with each one providing yet another fascinating piece of the puzzle that makes up our complex souls. Some of these points suggest that there needs to be far greater depth to our work if we are to receive the full effects of being in cosmic alignment. Their meanings show us that, beyond our human experience of life, there is also a higher soul mission we need to fulfill. When we are working with our deeper soul-level motivations, we are more likely to be successful in our endeavors than we would be if we were merely matching up our job title with our human-level skills, experience, or education level. To get started, let's explore a few points that provide the most major indicators of what your higher soul mission is.

The North and South Nodes: The Path of Destiny

Sometimes when you are making choices about where to focus next on your path, you may feel like you are being pulled in two different directions. When you tune into your inner knowing, you can hear the voice of the old you, which feels comfortable and safe. But you can also see the opposite possibility: realizing a new version of yourself by trying a totally new approach. The North and South Nodes of the Moon signify the path we must take to move from relying on expressing skills that are already familiar from the past toward realizing our higher destined path.

The South Node of Past Karma shows where we natural draw upon behaviors, skills, and talents we have already honed in a past life. We may have even done too much of these things to the detriment of our own growth. Always directly opposite the South Node on your chart, the North Node of Future Destiny refers to your greater potential for growth and reaching a new milestone in your soul lessons.

By pursuing the North Node path, you raise your energetic frequency, which allows you to manifest more of your desires much more quickly than if you relied on your past-life experience alone. It is like a shortcut to success, but it is not an easy ride because you still have to be willing to grow. Although we may think we are afraid to go after our greater potential because we might fail, there is usually a far deeper and more hidden fear of what could happen if we succeed.

At first, it may seem like we are harmlessly harnessing our true talents to our advantage when we channel our energy into our South Node, but this path cannot ever bring true fulfillment. When we challenge ourselves to learn new skills and develop new talents that are in alignment with our North Node, we not only expand our view of ourselves and the world but also become available for bigger and better opportunities. Look for the lasso symbol with the rounded curve pointing up for your North Node of Future Destiny and for the lasso with the rounded curve pointing down for the South Node talents you are meant to stop relying on for greater soul-led success.

If you see an "r" or "Rx" next to your North and South Nodes, that is because they are always in retrograde on everyone's chart. They refer to the nodal axis of the Moon where the Moon's orbit crosses the Earth's orbit around the Sun. The nodes are not physical objects but mathematically calculated points that always move backward (clockwise) on the wheel according to the lunar tilt.

NORTH NODE IN ARIES / SOUTH NODE IN LIBRA

Those who have their North Node in Aries are learning how to put themselves first. They step into their greater potential when they leave people-pleasing behind and instead seek to lift others up by protecting their boundaries and pouring their time and energy into their personal passions. By embracing their separate identity, they free themselves of the guilt of the past that has caused them to put their own desires aside. Then they can truly be there for others.

NORTH NODE IN TAURUS / SOUTH NODE IN SCORPIO

Those who have their North Node in Taurus need to learn to savor the process of pursuing their goals. Although they are intensely driven to create a more stable, serene future, the most rewarding outcome will come from being more cautious and slowing down. Instead of cutting corners to break out of the discomfort of not yet being where they want to be, they step into their greater potential when they focus instead on producing something that is of high quality as they learn to tap into their own sense of inner calm.

NORTH NODE IN GEMINI / SOUTH NODE IN SAGITTARIUS

The soul lesson for those with their North Node in Gemini surrounds the need to become more comfortable collaborating and sharing ideas with others. They may feel misunderstood or like others won't be interested in what they have to say. However, the more they can break down their ideas and present them in a simpler way, the more they will step into their greater potential and the more others will become receptive. This placement also points to a need to stop escaping from their problems and learn to better communicate their needs.

NORTH NODE IN CANCER / SOUTH NODE IN CAPRICORN

People with their North Node in Cancer are meant to learn to have greater compassion. Although they may be serious and driven to attain success in their work, it is through cultivating warmth in their personal relationships that they will succeed the most as a soul. Instead of focusing so much on earning money and receiving recognition, they will step into their greater potential when focusing on nurturing and being there for others.

NORTH NODE IN LEO / SOUTH NODE IN AQUARIUS

Those who have their North Node in Leo are meant to become powerful leaders and role models. Instead of focusing on progressing society as a whole, they step into their greater potential when they allow their originality to shine forth so that others can witness what's possible. By letting go of the need to cater to others' needs, they learn to stand confidently in their own spotlight as they aim to express their unique ideas.

NORTH NODE IN VIRGO / SOUTH NODE IN PISCES

Stepping out of their daydreams and into the real world is where those who have their North Node in Virgo will find their greater potential. Rather than hoping everything magically works out, they must learn to bring order and logic toward the pursuit of reaching their goals. As they learn it is not enough to simply wish for something, they achieve greater success by taking a more detail-oriented and hands-on approach.

NORTH NODE IN LIBRA / SOUTH NODE IN ARIES

Someone with the North Node in Libra is learning to be less focused on themselves and more in tune with the needs and desires of others. They are here to learn that they can get much further in life when they ask for help and cooperate with others. They step into their greater potential when they take more time to include others in their decisions instead of impulsively pushing forward with whatever they personally want to do.

NORTH NODE IN SCORPIO / SOUTH NODE IN TAURUS

People with their North Node in Scorpio are here to learn to stop getting in their own way and move more quickly in the direction of their desires. Instead of getting stuck in their old ways, Scorpio energy invites them to become more comfortable with the prospect of change and reinvention. As they strategize a plan to work smarter rather than harder to reach their personal goals, they step into their greater potential.

NORTH NODE IN SAGITTARIUS / SOUTH NODE IN GEMINI

The greatest potential for those born with the North Node in Sagittarius lies in getting away from the noise of the crowd and pursuing their own individual curiosities. This sign is here to learn to stop following the opinions of others and develop their own set of beliefs. Instead of being limited by the people and ideas who surround them, they succeed the most when they can go off on their own to dive deeply into their own interests regardless of the views of others.

NORTH NODE IN CAPRICORN / SOUTH NODE IN CANCER

Those who have their North Node in Capricorn step into their destined path when they learn to stop letting their emotions get in the way of achieving their long-term goals. Instead of focusing so much on taking care of others, they are here to become more self-sufficient. By honing their sense of discipline and drive to succeed in their work or career, they can gain powerful recognition that ends up helping and impacting many more people than they could if they were distracted by the drama of their personal relationships.

NORTH NODE IN AQUARIUS / SOUTH NODE IN LEO

Someone with the North Node in Aquarius is meant to stop hogging the spotlight or focusing too much on standing out and trying to come out on top as the best. Instead, it is when they focus on using their talents to improve the lives of others by being attuned to the needs of their community that they will receive greater fulfillment and success. They step into their greater potential when they seek to raise others up to their same level instead of aiming to put themselves on a pedestal.

NORTH NODE IN PISCES / SOUTH NODE IN VIRGO

The soul lesson for people with a North Node in Pisces surrounds the idea of being less critical toward themselves and others. They are here to learn to focus less on criticizing their mistakes and to let things go when they are not perfect. They step into their greater potential when they choose to have faith in the universe and believe in their dreams, knowing that keeping themselves attuned to the bigger purpose is more important than how they handle the smaller details.

The Nodes in the Houses

To step into your highest potential, you will need to...

North Node in the 1st House of
Identity, Authenticity, and Leadership:
Focus more on yourself and your own desires and less on helping
others in the way they need most.

North Node in the 2nd House of Values, Desires, and Goal Setting:
Stop working so hard to hustle for success and focus
on boosting up what is already going well in your life
to manifest more of what you crave.

North Node in the 3rd House of Social Networking:
Share your beliefs and experiences in a way that others can easily
access, use, and comprehend instead of hiding what you know for
fear of being misunderstood.

North Node in the 4th House of
Home, Family, and Long-term Security:
Create nourishing relationships and support systems
in your personal life instead of working so hard for
career recognition and public success.

North Node in the 5th House of Fun and Creativity:
Channel your self-expression into projects that are fun
for you to create rather than focusing so much on
what the audience wants you to do.

**North Node in the 6th House of
Health, Work, and Daily Rituals:**
Become more meticulous about reaching your
goals and supporting your physical needs instead of just
daydreaming about the future you crave.

**North Node in the 7th House of
Relationships and One-on-one Work:**
Put others' wants and needs above your own instead of being so
focused on developing yourself.

**North Node in the 8th House of
Business, Finance, and Shadow Work:**
Strategize a solid way to reach your goals based on logic rather than
hanging back and hoping that success will magically manifest.

**North Node in the 9th House of
Education, Exploration, and Self-discovery:**
Explore your own individual interests and curiosities instead of
polling others about what they think you should do.

North Node in the 10th House of
Career and Higher Calling:

Allow your talents to become recognized so you can make a
powerful impact in your work instead of making your personal and
home life your primary concern.

North Node in the 11th House of
Friendship and Community Outreach:

Embrace a more community-oriented approach
to creating things that add value to the lives of others
instead of only doing what you think is fun.

North Node in the 12th House of
Spirituality and Higher Purpose:

Have faith in the power of being connected to a bigger purpose
instead of obsessing over the tiny, imperfect details of everyday life.

Chiron: Unblocking Fears and Finding Your Healing Gift

When it comes to reaching greater heights in both our material success and our spiritual growth, we are usually the ones who hold ourselves back the most. When there are fears clouding our vision, we may not put ourselves out there to achieve our dreams, especially if we believe something terrible will happen to us if we fail. We often do not even realize we are doing this self-sabotaging behavior to ourselves because these psychological patterns of self-doubt run so deep. Luckily, there is a point on your chart you can consult to better understand where these fears come from, how to overcome them, and even how to turn them into a healing gift.

On the astrology chart, Chiron shows us where we are harboring an unhealed wound that may cause us to do extreme things to protect ourselves out of mistrust and fear. Because we do not wish to repeat painful lessons from past lives, we avoid conflict in certain aspects of life to keep from re-opening the wound. The only way to heal from these issues is to face what you are the most afraid of and prove to yourself that, even if you do fail, you will be completely safe and okay.

Another reason it can be powerful to channel your energy into the aspect of yourself highlighted by Chiron is that it shows where you have a natural ability to help bring healing to others. Look for the symbol that looks like a K on top of an O to find the key to unlocking the deep healing that will bring a greater sense of wholeness to your soul and others' souls.

CHIRON IN ARIES

Those who were born with Chiron in Aries may be afraid of asserting themselves, standing up for themselves, and becoming an independent force of nature in the world. As they learn that it is okay if others are not as enthusiastic about their ideas as they are, they learn to heal a fear of being separated or alone. Their greatest healing gift is their ability to show others how to embrace their own passions regardless of what anyone else may think of them.

CHIRON IN TAURUS

Someone with Chiron in Taurus may be afraid to express what they want or need in life, whether it is love, money, or something else they value or require. This is because they may feel like they would not be supported even if they asked. As they work to realize that they are deserving of receiving all their desires, they develop a powerful healing ability to make others feel more confident about getting what they need.

CHIRON IN GEMINI

Chiron in Gemini's wound centers around feeling unincluded in others' conversations. The prospect of having to share their ideas may bring up memories of times when their voice was not valued or understood. Although they may not feel like what they have to say is worthy of being shared, the more they speak up and express their expertise, the more they gain the ability to heal and inspire others to step up and share their thoughts and beliefs too.

CHIRON IN CANCER

Chiron in Cancer has a deep block around allowing others to nurture them. They may have felt abandoned by the people who were meant to care for them in the past, so they avoid opening up to share their true feelings with others. At the same time, they easily make others feel nourished and supported. When they begin to let other people in on their innermost concerns, they help heal the world and show others it is safe to let other people take care of them.

CHIRON IN LEO

Those who have Chiron in Leo have a block around allowing their true talents to be seen or witnessed. They may be afraid to stand out as someone who is the best at what they do because that type of attention may have attracted a painful experience in the past. Their healing gift becomes activated the more they put themselves out there and show others it is safe to confidently claim the spotlight and let their gifts shine.

CHIRON IN VIRGO

Chiron in Virgo has a wound to heal that centers around fearing the development of ailments in the physical body or the impulse to control small and seemingly insignificant details to their detriment. They may have an especially strong fear of failure, which results in them either being overly obsessive with every detail or not wanting to attempt their goals at all. As they work to overcome their own fears of imperfection, they bring healing to others by helping them learn to love and accept themselves exactly as they already are.

CHIRON IN LIBRA

Chiron in Libra may doubt that they have anything of any value to offer to another person. Fearing that others may not appreciate their help, they can block themselves from forming meaningful relationships or asking for what they want from others when they need support. As they work to see things from others' perspectives and trust the intuitive hints they receive in social situations, they gain a healing gift that allows them to help others bring balance to their relationships as well.

CHIRON IN SCORPIO

With Chiron in Scorpio, the deeper need for healing comes from a fear of being powerless. They may worry about losing the things they love to an extreme level that they feel grief even when there is no outside indication that the loss will happen. The more they learn to trust themselves and let go of the worries and concerns that do not serve them, the more they develop a healing ability that allows them to help others feel empowered to create important changes in their lives.

CHIRON IN SAGITTARIUS

Chiron in Sagittarius is here to learn to rely on themselves for answers instead of taking others' advice at face value. Skeptical of anyone who claims to be a teacher or guru, they are meant to discover their own personal beliefs without being influenced by another person's authority. This sign provides healing to others when they help them tune out what religious, spiritual, or cultural teachings say they must do and create their own authentic, freedom-filled life path.

CHIRON IN CAPRICORN

Those who are born with Chiron in Capricorn are afraid of living a chaotic life, so they may go out of their way to try to control situations that are not theirs to control. Often blaming themselves when things go wrong or somehow do not satisfy their extremely high standards, they are here to learn how to put less pressure on themselves and celebrate every small effort. Their healing gift involves their ability to teach others to become more balanced in going after their goals.

CHIRON IN AQUARIUS

Chiron in Aquarius's greatest fear revolves around being rejected or pushed out of their community or circle of friends. Worrying that they are too different from others, they may back away from forming social connections or go out of their way to pretend they are someone else in order to please others. As they push through these fears and honor the value they can bring to others, they help heal others by providing them with a sense of belonging.

CHIRON IN PISCES

People with Chiron in Pisces may feel that they are always the victim. They fear that the universe does not have their best interests in mind and may feel that everyone is out to get them. As they learn they do not have to suffer through life, they develop the gift of giving others greater faith in the supportive nature of the universe and the teaching that our reality is created based on our beliefs.

Chiron in the Houses

Your greatest need for healing and strongest ability to heal others centers around...

Chiron in the 1st House of Identity, Authenticity, and Leadership:
Gaining confidence in how you show up in the world as your most authentic self.

Chiron in the 2nd House of Values, Desires, and Goal Setting:
Being clear with others about what you really want and need and asking for help in reaching your goals.

Chiron in the 3rd House of Social Networking:
Speaking up and allowing your thoughts, ideas, and opinions to be heard even if you fear others won't understand you.

Chiron in the 4th House of Home, Family, and Long-term Security:
Forming stronger bonds with your family and being there for others without allowing their needs to overtake yours.

Chiron in the 5th House of Fun and Creativity:
Allowing your unique talents to shine forth as you have more fun sharing your creativity and originality with the world.

Chiron in the 6th House of Health, Work, and Daily Rituals:
Accepting and loving yourself just as you are, even if your health,
home, work, or habits are not perfect.

Chiron in the 7th House of Relationships and One-on-one Work:
Prioritizing your personal needs in relationships instead of putting
the other person ahead of you.

**Chiron in the 8th House of
Business, Finance, and Shadow Work:**
Becoming empowered by looking beneath the surface of your
financial or emotional insecurities.

**Chiron in the 9th House of
Education, Exploration, and Self-discovery:**
Seeking out your own sense of meaning and being your own guru
rather than relying on others to tell you how to live your life.

Chiron in the 10th House of Career and Higher Calling:
Appreciating yourself for every small achievement you make instead
of letting the fear of never being recognized take over your life.

Chiron in the 11th House of Friendship and Community Outreach:
Overcoming a fear of rejection or conformity to create a true sense
of belonging in your community.

Chiron in the 12th House of Spirituality and Higher Purpose:
Trusting in the divine support of the universe and not feeling like a
victim to your circumstances.

Pallas Athena: Your Soul's Inspiration

One of the more uncommon and often misunderstood asteroids, Pallas Athena helps us tap into the glimmer of serendipity that makes us feel like magic really does exist. Through my research, I have come to know Pallas Athena as the goddess of spiritual wisdom and soul-deep inspiration. This asteroid signifies what makes the world light up in pure magic for us based on the inspiring influence we can pass on to others. When we are able to see evidence of our work's ability to positively affect others, it makes all of our efforts feel all the more special and rewarding. We finally feel like we have found our magic.

How to look up Pallas Athena:

1. Go to www.astro.com.
2. From the top menu, go to Free Horoscopes > Drawings & Calculations > Extended Chart Selection.
3. Click on, "click here to go to the data entry page." Then enter in your birth information in the form and choose Continue.
4. In the last section at the bottom of the Extended Chart Selection page, look for the Additional Objects section. This where you can highlight "Pallas" from the list of asteroids. Then select "Click here to show the chart."
5. Once the chart comes up, look for the diamond-shaped symbol that resembles a shield with a cross at the bottom. This is your Pallas Athena!

Another way to look up Pallas Athena is by going to ww.uraniaday.com/urania-calculator. Enter your birth information and choose Pallas under the Asteroid dropdown. You can also find this symbol by getting the paid pro version of AstroApp at www.astroapp.com and selecting Pallas Athena's shield-like symbol in the settings.

PALLAS ATHENA IN ARIES

Pallas Athena in Aries feels lit up when they are motivating and igniting others to take action and bring new ideas to life faster and with less hesitation. They love to see others become more enthusiastic in pursuing their true passions and asserting themselves as powerful individuals who are in charge of their own lives. They gain spiritual wisdom by being a cheerleader and helping others get excited about new ideas.

PALLAS ATHENA IN TAURUS

Life feels the most magical for those with Pallas Athena in Taurus when they are supporting others in feeling calmer, more stable, and serene. Being able to create a sense of steadiness so they can give themselves everything they need also brings a sense of peace and wonder. They can tune into their magic by sharing what is most pleasing to their senses and using it to help ground others.

PALLAS ATHENA IN GEMINI

Pallas Athena in Gemini loves to pick up random bits of information from the world around them. This sign feels most attuned to the magical forces of the universe when they are able to pass along key information that has been proven to positively change others' lives. They also pride themselves on forming meaningful connections with others from many walks of life and then helping those people form connections with each other.

PALLAS ATHENA IN CANCER

For Pallas Athena in Cancer, magic reveals itself when they are creating a comfortable foundation or space in which others feel safe to express their true selves and confide in them for protection and healing. They have access to an even deeper level of intuitive and spiritual wisdom than most, and their empathetic nature allows them to easily tune into the deeper needs of others. Most of all, they love to feel appreciated and needed.

PALLAS ATHENA IN LEO

With Pallas Athena in Leo, bringing the best out in others is what brings magic to their life. They love to encourage others to more boldly and confidently express their creative talents and ideas. Although they are quite proud of the attentive effort they put into their own creative work, they ultimately feel most rewarded spiritually when they can generously pass along their example to help another person shine.

PALLAS ATHENA IN VIRGO

Pallas Athena in Virgo feels connected to spiritual wisdom when they are working to attain a sense of purity or perfectionism in a project they are doing for other people. For them, being of service and helping others remove what is not working, refine their vision, or put their life together in a more sensible order feels like a magical experience. They most appreciate when they can contribute to the smaller details that make up a greater whole.

PALLAS ATHENA IN LIBRA

Pallas Athena in Libra loves to luxuriate in life and take in all the beauty they can from the world around them. A greater sense of spiritual connection permeates into their reality when they can share this sense of peace, justice, or harmony with others. They find their magic from supporting others in lightening up and finding greater enjoyment in all that is special about life.

PALLAS ATHENA IN SCORPIO

Pallas Athena in Scorpio loves to help others uncover their deeper mysteries. With an intensely strong intuition, they have a knack for unlocking what is hidden behind others' insecurities and fears. They tune into spiritual wisdom when helping others create a change or transformation so they can pursue their true passions in a way that brings them empowerment. Reinvention is their brand of magic.

PALLAS ATHENA IN SAGITTARIUS

Guiding others to find their own answers is what brings Pallas Athena in Sagittarius a feeling of oneness with their own spiritual wisdom. They naturally love to share what they have learned about the deeper meaning of life to help others expand their perspective and grow. However, the true feeling of magic arrives when they are assisting others in discovering and authentically aligning with their own inner path.

PALLAS ATHENA IN CAPRICORN

Pallas Athena in Capricorn has a special gift for putting all the steps to an important goal into a perfectly ordered system. They are even able to identify what challenges may arise in the future to avoid falling into potential pitfalls. A sense of being connected to spiritual wisdom arises for them when they can see or experience how incredibly impactful their organizational framework is for others.

PALLAS ATHENA IN AQUARIUS

Pallas Athena in Aquarius receives spiritual wisdom in the form of random strokes of genius. They have a forward-thinking perspective of the world that allows them to easily see beyond the limits of convention. They find their magic when they can use their unusually cutting-edge interests or seemingly strange or new-age ideas to help others liberate themselves from a complicated problem that is affecting the community at large.

PALLAS ATHENA IN PISCES

Work feels most magical to Pallas Athena in Pisces when they are helping others tap into their own magic by sharing their creative, intuitive, spiritual, or philosophical ponderings. Dreamy and compassionate, they feel at one with their spiritual wisdom when others are clearly inspired by their ideas. Their strong imagination helps them envision exciting potential possibilities, which they can then help others tune into for themselves, too.

Pallas Athena in the Houses

The world comes alive in pure magic for you when you are...

Pallas Athena in the 1st House of
Identity, Authenticity, and Leadership:
Being appreciated and recognized simply for
being your most authentic self.

Pallas Athena in the 2nd House of
Values, Desires, and Goal Setting:
Encouraging others to believe in their ability to manifest their
dreams, goals, and desires.

Pallas Athena in the 3rd House of Social Networking:
Sharing ideas and messages that make others' lives noticeably better
or connecting people to form a supportive network.

Pallas Athena in the 4th House of
Home, Family, and Long-term Security:
Holding space for others to air their emotions and
feel seen, heard, and cared for.

Pallas Athena in the 5th House of Fun and Creativity:
Coming up with fun, creative, and original ideas that others enjoy
and encouraging others to express their creativity, too.

Pallas Athena in the 6th House of
Health, Work, and Daily Rituals:
Serving others to help them create better daily habits that increase
their overall wellbeing.

Pallas Athena in the 7th House of
Relationships and One-on-one Work:
Helping others on an individual basis and witnessing the powerful changes they are making due to your personalized support.

Pallas Athena in the 8th House of
Business, Finance, and Shadow Work:
Helping others take ownership over their time and money or dive deep to uncover hidden blocks.

Pallas Athena in the 9th House of
Education, Exploration, and Self-discovery:
Expanding others' view of what is possible by sharing guidance gained from personal experience.

Pallas Athena in the 10th House of
Career and Higher Calling:
Using your career efforts and public image to make a powerful impact on the lives of people you have never even met.

Pallas Athena in the 11th House of
Friendship and Community Outreach:
Improving the world by bringing people together to find better solutions to widespread challenges.

Pallas Athena in the 12th House of
Spirituality and Higher Purpose:
Helping others connect with their higher purpose or mission by releasing their fears and limiting beliefs.

CHAPTER 5

The Bigger Picture

Over the last few chapters, you have decoded each of the different points on your chart. With so many aspects of yourself now revealed, you may find that they all seem quite separate when you look at each of the individual interpretations on their own. To get a more cohesive understanding of your cosmic calling, it is important to take a step back and look at the bigger picture of how all the unique elements of your calling weave together.

Bringing It All Together

To integrate all you have learned about yourself, start by taking an intuitive inventory of how your chart compares with your current life.

* **Where have your dreams, ideas, and passions been validated?** Compare what you have learned to your current interests.
* **Where are you still missing out on expressing certain aspects of yourself?** Perhaps there are things about yourself you already knew but that you have not yet allowed to come out into the light through your work.
* **What aspects of your calling are still confusing to you?** You may not yet have enough experience with these aspects to know exactly how they are meant to be expressed.

Astrology is an energetic language. Therefore, there can be many different ways to interpret and express what you have learned. Your chart can seem like an abstract concept if not everything makes sense to you right away. On the flip side, it may be eerie how much sense it makes. The difference depends on how much soul searching and self-awareness work you have already done.

Although astrology provides the framework of your blueprint, it's still up to you to fill in the story and continue to explore. Think of it as a map. A map provides the directions to go to get what you want, but you never know what experiences will be waiting for you along the way unless you physically go. Aim to keep an open mind as you continue to watch out for and explore these different avenues of your psyche. After sorting through what type of work feels most inspiring to you, you might extract even more clues when you come back to explore your chart again later on.

Noticing Repeating Chart Patterns

Another way to clarify your calling and to bring your newfound inspirations down to earth is by zooming out to look at your chart as a whole. See if you notice any interesting patterns that are emerging. For example, you may have a group of planets or points all in the same sign or house. This would put an extra emphasis on those energies. Therefore, they are especially important for you to express as part of your life's work.

If you have three or more points in a sign or house, it is referred to as a *stellium*. On my chart, I have five planets that form a stellium in the sign of Capricorn, which emphasizes that I am meant to be a teacher and someone who creates set paths for others to follow to achieve their goals. If you have multiple points in a particular house, it suggests an especially strong need to develop and express your skills in that area of life.

You may also notice that your chart says the same thing in different ways. For example, one point could tell you that you love to learn and share your ideas while another explains that you are here to be a messenger or guide. It is common for many points in different areas of the chart to bring home the same or a similar idea. When that happens, it makes your calling easier to find.

If your planets and points are scattered all around the wheel or if there are conflicting messages coming from the different areas you are interpreting, that means there are many different directions you could go. One theory is that you have chosen a more challenging life to help you grow. There is nothing wrong with being a multi-dimensional and, therefore, multi-passionate person, but you may need to take longer to explore your differing interests to find a way to bring them all together into one project or path. Don't worry. It is still more than possible if you stick with it!

When in doubt over what your chart is trying to say, you can go through an integrative energetic realignment process by following the order of the hierarchy of the chart. First, seek to bring alignment into your life and work by focusing on fully expressing and supporting the essence of your Sun. Then look for ways to nourish yourself better by harnessing your Moon. As you go in the order of the points listed in this book, make some changes to how you express your energy in your work until you have found a way to fully express each aspect of your soul's essence in the way that feels best.

Understanding Planetary Relationships

Another way to determine how each of the planets plays a role in your self-expression is to pick apart the relationships the planets and points have with one another. Think of each of the planets and points as having its own unique power source. While Mars rules over the energy of action and drive, Venus has a softer and more receptive energy. What happens when they are on opposite sides of the chart and they are both vying for your attention in different areas at the same time or inside the same person? It signifies a greater need to find balance.

An *aspect* is the technical name for the connections that the different planets make based on the angle they reside in comparison to each other on a chart. It is like they are always having unique conversations with each other based on how far apart they are. This is a more advanced and meticulous way to use astrology that is based on complex geometry, but if you take the time to sort through it, you can uncover even more helpful clues about your hidden quirks. Aspects can also explain why you may sometimes have trouble accessing or expressing particular sides of yourself. It could be that they are affected by another planet's powerful pull.

Depending on where you get your chart, the aspects may be shown as different-colored lines right in the center of the wheel or there may be a grid in the shape of half of a pyramid in the corner with symbols in it. Each of these symbols denotes a different type of geometrical angle, which will have a different energetic effect on the planets or points that are involved. They are listed here in order of their strength. Keep in mind that the planets also vary in their gravitational strength. The further away a planet is in the solar system, the more weight and power it has.

 Conjunction: The energies blend together, so their interpretations can be read individually as well as combined.

For example:

* *Venus conjunct Neptune* means you especially value your dream vision.
* *Mercury conjunct Pluto* means you have an intense and probing mind.
* *Venus conjunct your Sun* means you express yourself best by bringing love and beauty to others.

Square: The energies are fighting against each other, bringing tension and a challenge to grow and up-level.

For example:

* ✺ *Mercury square Pluto* means you will have to face your fears to communicate your message.
* ✺ *Moon square Neptune* means you will have to step out of your comfort zone to realize your dreams in life.
* ✺ *Mars square Saturn* means you will need to overcome a craving for instant gratification to achieve your goals.

Opposition: The energies oppose each other and require a balance of your time and energy in expressing each one.

For example:

* ✺ *Neptune opposite Chiron* means you will need to overcome past wounds to create the world you want to live in.
* ✺ *Jupiter opposite Saturn* means you will need to balance exciting opportunities with hard work and discipline.

Trine: The energies flow harmoniously and bring extra support to one another.

For example:

* ✺ *Sun trine Jupiter* means you are especially optimistic and excitable.

* *Mercury trine Pluto* means you have a very probing mind that is not afraid to dive deep into uncomfortable subjects.

Sextile: Similar to but not as strong as a trine, the energies bring pleasing opportunities to each other.

For example:

* *Venus sextile Pluto* means you enjoy growing, transforming, and up-leveling.
* *Mars sextile Saturn* means you are goal-driven and proactive.

Quincunx: The energies will require some adjustments or compromises to be made because the signs they are in are so different in nature.

For example:

* *Mercury quincunx Jupiter* means you will need to continually adjust how you share your ideas to stay excited.
* *Sun quincunx Saturn* means you will need to continually adjust your behavior, focus, and actions to achieve your long-term goals.

Don't worry if this technique isn't making sense to you. It is just an additional layer of information you can explore if you want to dive deeper and if it happens to call to you!

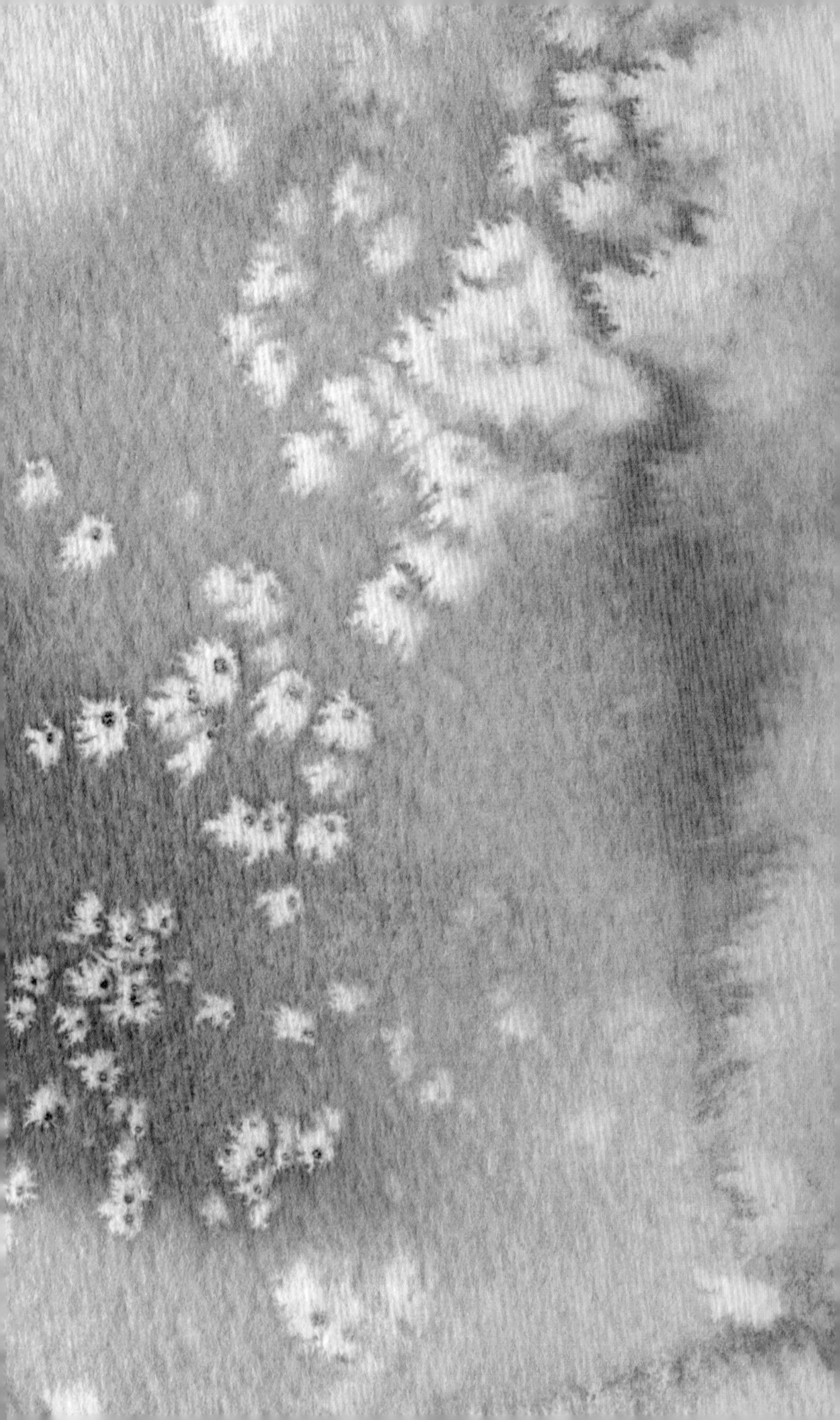

CHAPTER 6

All in Divine Timing

You may be either relieved or disappointed to know that there are times in life when we are simply not meant to understand the exact path to follow to pursue our higher calling. It can be frustrating when inspiration and clarity are just not coming, even when you are trying so hard to get to know yourself and explore the ways you can express your true talents to be of greater service to the world. If you are still feeling unclear about aspects of your calling, it may not yet be time for you to fully know. We blossom into who we are meant to become at exactly the right time, and it is the many unique experiences we gather along the way that contribute to our greater understanding when it all finally comes together for us.

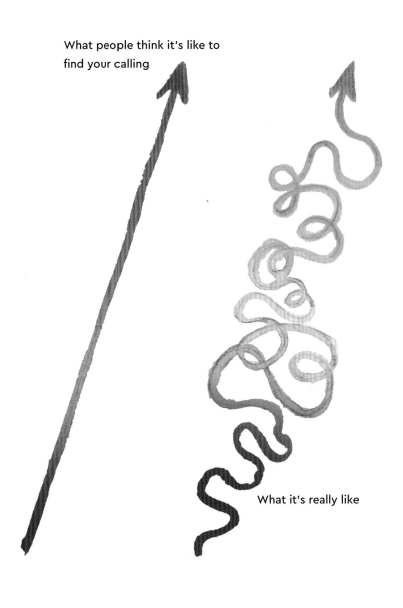

What people think it's like to
find your calling

What it's really like

Trusting in Yourself and Your Timeline

In addition to reading our personal charts, we can track the timing of the events that are meant to happen in our lives by following the paths of the planets in the sky. As the planets move around the wheel in real time, they form connections with the planets on our charts. When this happens, they trigger different aspects of us to change and evolve, all in divine timing.

There will be a time when it all comes together for you in your life's work. This usually occurs when the planets enter the part of the sky that correlates with your 10th House of Career and Higher Calling. Although the Sun, Mercury, Venus, and Mars will move into this area once every one to two years, bringing smaller hits of inspiration and ideas as they do, the planet that brings the biggest and most life-changing revelations around our true calling is Jupiter. When Jupiter moves through our 10th house every eleven to twelve years, we become filled with noticeably expansive and exciting inspiration for how we can use our special talents, passions, interests to benefit and impact the world. The day I first asked myself, "What if I just became an astrologer?" was the day this magical event happened for me.

How to look up when Jupiter will enter your 10th house:

1. Go to www.planetwatcher.com.
2. Look for the blue symbol for Jupiter on the wheel.
3. Using the month and year buttons at the top, keep pressing the date forward until you see Jupiter move into alignment with the same zodiac sign and the exact degree as your 10th house (or MC) on your chart.

Keep in mind that this may have already happened for you in the recent past. If so, you probably already know what you are meant to do, and now it is just a matter of building up the confidence to bring it out into the world. If it will still be a while until Jupiter moves into this area—perhaps even many years—don't lose heart. There are other areas of your life you can still work on improving and infusing your most authentic self into in the meantime, and this will help support you in stepping into your calling and doing your best work down the line.

As you have learned from this book, we are each special and unique. Do not try to compare your timeline to anyone else's. We all naturally move at our own pace, and so do the planets. There is no need to hustle, push, or hurry because there is plenty of time to step into who you really are and what you are meant to become. Trust that you will know when it is time for you to act regardless of the planets because you will naturally feel called and inspired to do exactly that.

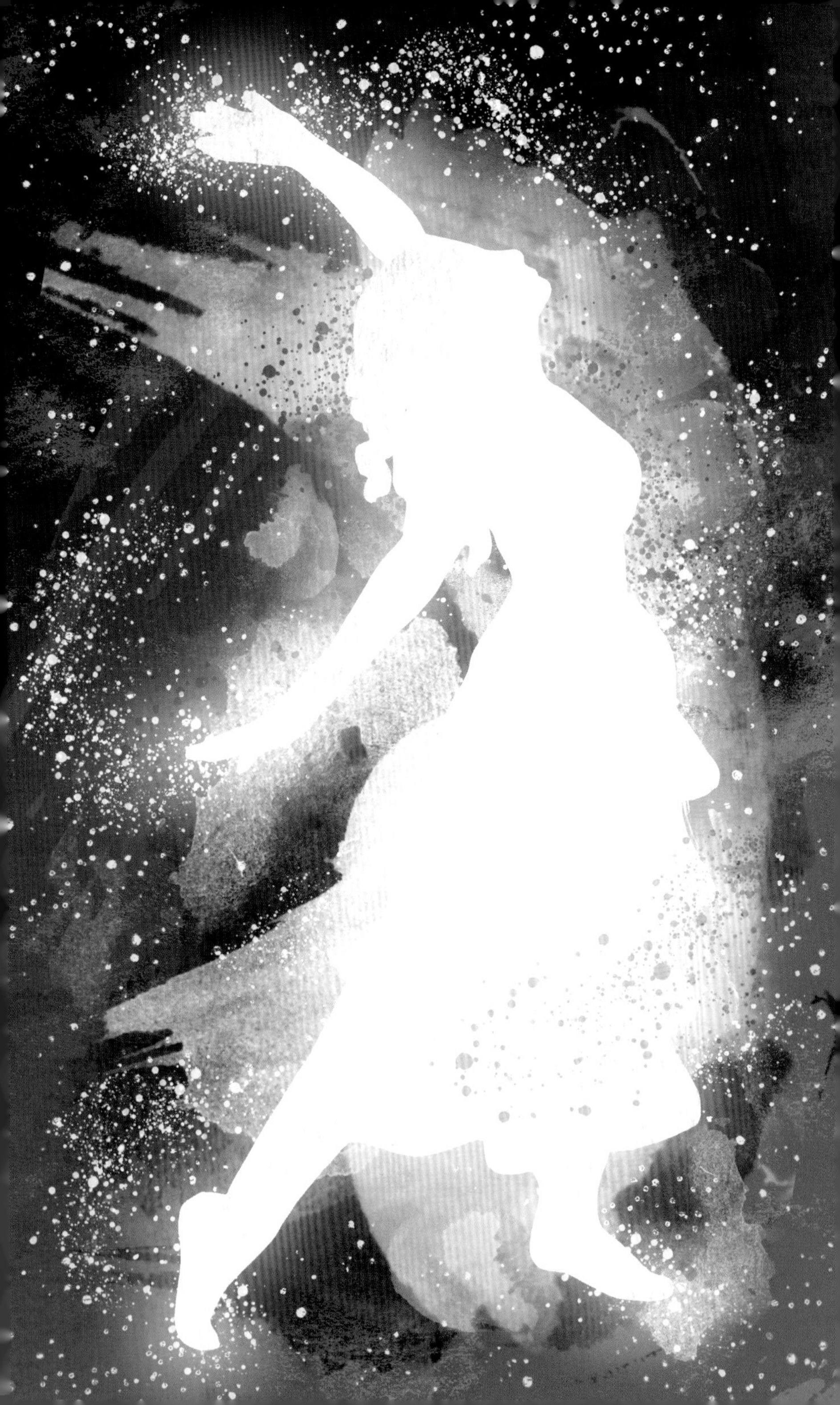

Embracing the Evolution of Your Soul Mission

Earlier, we discussed many different ways to express your calling. Chances are, you have already been living in alignment with your astrology chart without even knowing it, but over time you will learn how to express the energies of your inner workings in ways that feel even more aligned. Alignment feels like ease, flow, happiness, lightness, and excitement. What feels most aligned for you can change and evolve over time. As new insights and inspiration enter our minds, we pivot and shift to allow our ideas to evolve into something more.

It is more than okay for you to grow out of the things you used to love. It is safe for you to give up old versions of yourself and the titles, accolades, degrees, desires, and values that may have once felt aligned to you in the past. Change is one of the most natural parts of life, and it is never too late to make a shift, no matter how old you are or how much energy you have already put into your past work. No matter what you decide to go on and do, you will bring your past experiences and learnings with you as the foundation for your future growth.

Over time, I have been a retail worker; an office assistant; a clothing photographer for a fashion website; a graphic, magazine, and brand designer; an astrology reader; and a business coach. Today I am a teacher and now an author. I still remember when each of these new levels felt incredibly exciting and most aligned. I also remember when each one felt scary to let go of as I stepped into the next iteration of myself as I followed where my soul felt called to go.

Change can be scary at first, but when the reward involves stepping into a freer, lighter, and more authentic version of you, you can never really go wrong! The ideal work situation will feel fun and exciting. You won't have to push yourself to pursue it because you will feel pulled or, rather, called.

Next Step: Go for It!

It can be fun to learn about yourself with astrology, but please don't let this be another book you let sit on your shelf without integrating the information into your life. You and your calling are far too important for that. You were wired and born to do amazing things. The planets can help, but because of free will, it is still up to you to take action. This world needs your magic, and there are people out there waiting for you to step up and share the unique blend of skills and talents you possess in the way that only you can. All you have to do is be willing to answer the call.

As you move forward from here, try to see every step you take in the direction of your calling as a curious experiment. Move into greater alignment with your newfound self-awareness by taking one small, inspired action step at a time. There is nothing you can do to mess it up and no mistake that cannot be fixed. See yourself as a mad scientist in a lab, seeking to find what works and what does not as you make small shifts to how you express your energy and share your gifts. Which experiments feel good, and which fall flat? You won't know what will truly work for you until you get out there and give it a try.

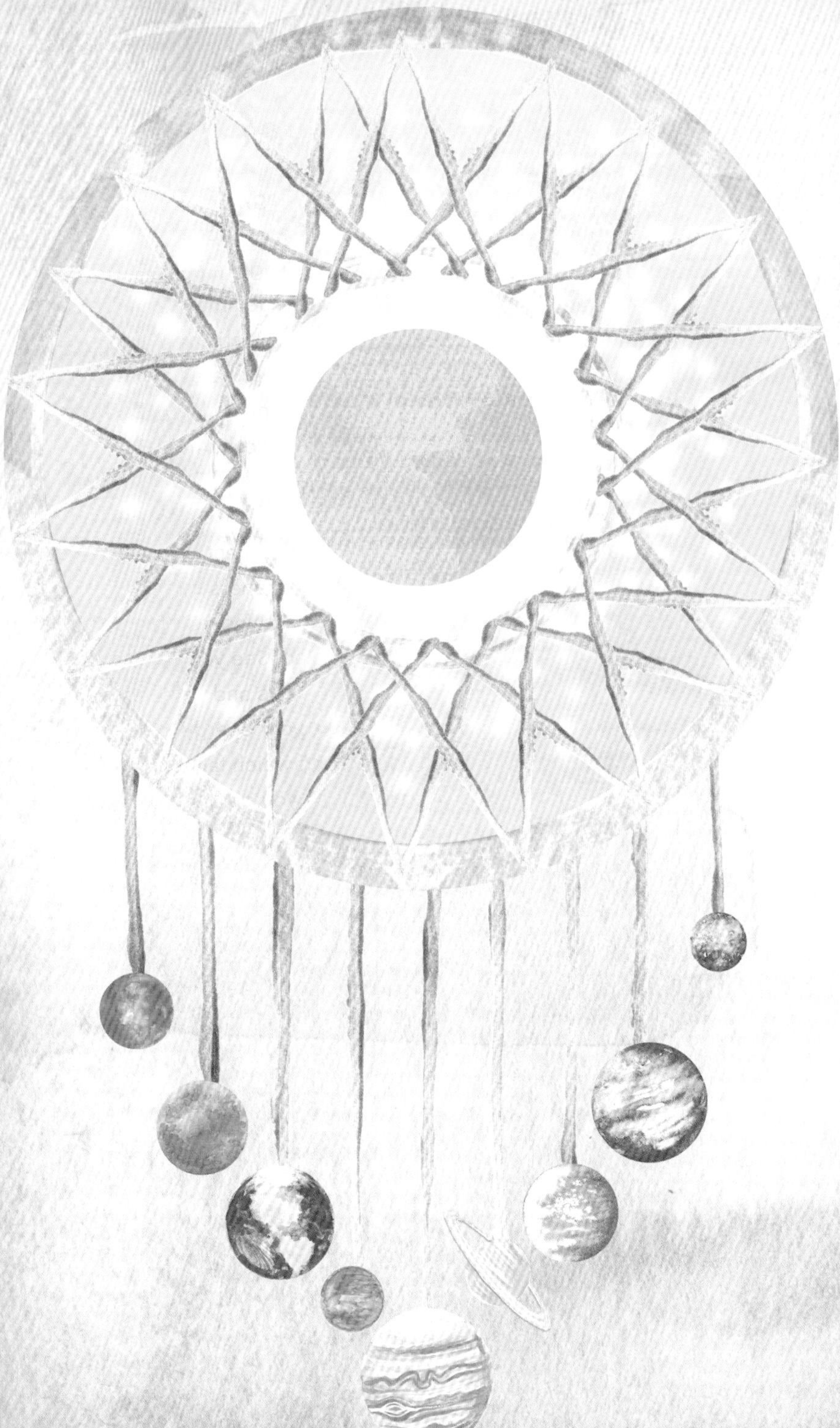

Chart Symbology

PLANETARY ASPECTS

 Conjunction = The energies are blended together

 Square = The energies go up against each other

 Opposition = The energies oppose each other

 Sextile = The energies help each other out

 Trine = The energies flow harmoniously

Quincunx = The energies will require some adjustments to be made in your life

ASTRO SYMBOLS

 Sun

 Moon

 Mercury

 Venus

 Mars

Jupiter

Saturn

Uranus

Neptune

Pluto

North Node

South Node

 Rising Sign

 Midheaven (Career Line)

Chiron

Pallas Athena

ZODIAC SIGNS

♈ Aries   Leo   ♐ Sagittarius

♉ Taurus   Virgo   ♑ Capricorn

♊ Gemini   ♎ Libra   ♒ Aquarius

Cancer   Scorpio   ♓ Pisces

THE HOUSE SYSTEM

1 Identity, Authenticity & Leadership

2 Values, Desires & Goal Setting

3 Social Networking

4 Home, Family & Long-term Security

5 Fun & Creativity

6 Health, Work & Daily Rituals

7 Relationships & One-on-one Work

8 Business, Finance & Shadow Work

9 Education, Exploration & Self-discovery

10 Career & Higher Calling

11 Friendship & Community Outreach

12 Spirituality & Higher Purpose

About the Author

Natalie Walstein is a full-time professional astrologer at Soulshine Astrology (www.soulshineastrology.com) and the host of The Cosmic Calling podcast. Since 2016, she has helped thousands of people around the world learn how to use their astrology chart to gain clarity and confidence on their career path so they can also go on to create powerful ripple effects for others by doing what they love through their work. She is based in Honolulu, Hawaii.

Acknowledgments

Thank you so much to everyone who has believed in me and my mission throughout the years, especially the thousands of clients, customers, podcast listeners, and readers who have cheered me on since the beginning as well as everyone on Team Soulshine. Huge thanks to my book team at Fair Winds Press, including editors Lydia Rasmussen and Jill Alexander, and everyone who has contributed their professional time and energy to support this dream. I'm especially grateful to my parents, Howard and Carolyn Walstein, who have always shown me how to shine my light brightly so that the people who need my help can find my work. Thank you also to all the coaches, colleagues, and mentors who have inspired me to believe in myself, to never settle for less, and to always dream bigger—you know who you are!

Index